HUMORESQUE

HUMORESQUE

TALES

FRANCESCO DE NIGRIS

authorHOUSE®

AuthorHouse™
1663 Liberty Drive
Bloomington, IN 47403
www.authorhouse.com
Phone: 1-800-839-8640

First published by AuthorHouse   06/06/2011

ISBN: 978-1-4567-8369-3 (sc)
ISBN: 978-1-4567-8370-9 (ebk)

Printed in the United States of America

Contents

The surprise

. . . .

THE DAY I HAD BEEN long waiting for eventually came. I clearly knew what was going to happen at the theatre that evening. Before leaving home, I rang a friend up to make sure to have a place to go, after. She was staying home because she had some work to finish off, she said. I asked her whether I might come over later on, and she answered she would be pleased.

I hung up the phone.

Chance was offering to me such an occasion, I knew it would not turn up once again. My old fellow was coming back to his town preceded by his fame, by the esteem of the people who had seen him, an infant prodigy, take up the career as international concert artist, just as many had prophesied for him. How many times, in all these years, I had seen the scenes of this movie with the eyes of my imagination.

As a matter of fact, that evening the Maestro was going to perform before the audience of his hometown, and everybody was sure it would be a success. I was going to acclaim him as well, no doubt about it.

The schedule included Mozart—almost an imperative for one who had studied in Salzburg—, Beethoven, Liszt. The city walls almost shouted that, entire walls were covered with posters, obsessively reminding me of my intention, the surprise. During some rare moments I did consider with clarity the absurdity of my purpose. I tried to convince myself to refrain, but now every doubt had vanished. I had to do that, that would be my triumph.

The plan was plain, even elementary. My seat at the theatre was close to the proscenium, second row of boxes, just over the piano: the pianist would master the keyboard while I would dominate them both from my place. It took just waiting.

I decided to make it happen during the performance of Liszt's Sonata, and I precisely calculated the exact moment. Even though the Sonata in B minor was out of reach for my ability, I knew by heart every one of its elements, I had analyzed its structure since the time I attended the conservatoire, during the lessons of History of music.

Due to my vast knowledge of the musical literature (I must say it with no arrogance or false modesty) I obtained the liking and the esteem of the teacher ho History. I became his favourite, arousing a series of inevitable envy and heavy allusions, just because he was suspected to be homosexual. Even if I instinctively knew that, I preferred to pay no attention to that.

After having looked at myself in the mirror for a long time, I went out. I as well gave a glance at the mirror in the lift, trying to relax and to avoid thinking too much.

I crossed a city invaded by cars, I swore while searching for a parking (not too far from the theatre, by the way) and on foot I got to the cinema-theatre "Roma", a most modest room with no history—movies on fourth release, variety show companies remembered by the old ones, some recent shy raid in the phantasmagoric world of hard-core.

I got through the crowd that blocked the hall of the theatre. I recognized some faces, some people recognized and greeted me, but on a purpose I did not linger chatting and directly went to my place. There, hidden in my seat, I hoped to be unnoticed. Maybe the people I had hurriedly greeted before had noticed my harmless appearance. This thought calmed me down. Nevertheless it was necessary to go unnoticed, thus the half-light of the box was very useful. I opened the booklet with the programme I had taken from a table in the hall, and I plunged deep into it.

While I was avidly reading through the biographical notes of the maestro, I had the illusory feeling that those notes were the report of my own brilliant career, which in fact I did not follow. It was not me anymore, but another myself coming to life in my imagination. Meanwhile, I kept on taking quick anxious looks in direction of the stage in the dark, and of the people entering in dribs and drabs to get to their seats. The bell rang three times to hurry the audience along to their places, the lights turned down, and the profiles drawing in the dark remained motionless and gathered themselves in a silence broken by some coughs and rustles of various intensity.

The pianist appeared after a few seconds. With studied steps he took his place at the piano. The stage was strangely in the dark. Some latecomers proceeded tentatively. Nervous coughs here and there. Murmuring. The pianist motionless in a rigidity that seemed to absorb him in a unique block with the piano, in the darkness that began to seem less intense. From my point of observation, at the top, I hypnotically stared at the dark figure.

The sight of a grand piano always brought to my mind somber, funereal images, especially in the dreams that frequently crowded some restless nights of mine. In my oneiric imagination, but daydreaming too, the piano's long tail turned into a shiny uncanny coffin. Thus the simple fact of playing a piano, of mastering it by means of the technique, deriving from this activity pleasure and exaltation, used to bring me in touch with death, with the anguish of death. In my dreams the piano turned into an instrument of destruction, of rancorous revenge. Mastering the instrument, thus, coincided with an unrestrained feeling of omnipotence, wanting to defeat the ineluctability of the dark void.

The darkness on the scene, which initially alarmed the public and looked like an oversight, a technical mistake, showed to be not accidental. On the wooden pavement some steps clearly spread breaking the half-light. It seemed as if a ghost had reached the pianist: he was waiting for it to start the performance. The newcomer reached for the lectern, put on it some papers and placed on the sides two lamps that lighted up immediately, spreading around an orange halo that reached the pianist's face, who still remained motionless, and the papers on the lectern.

The pianist cleared his throat and moved forwards. The two changed a glimpse of understanding.

A murmur of surprise raised up from the hall. The maestro was going to perform with the score under his eyes, and not playing by heart, as it was usual. I must admit that the innovation disoriented me: I could not tell whether the maestro wanted to create a private dimension, an intimate frame, a sort of lounge for few privileged, or, on the contrary, he wanted to show he took the audience in no consideration, maybe he wanted to perform for himself rather than for the avid expectations of a vulgar audience, all things considered. From my hiding place I could not help but receive that novelty sarcastically. I thought that the maestro's fame made the audience ready to accept this or any other extravagance, as if the halo that surrounded him were a powerful pass. I could imagine the audience subdued to the maestro with the same frightened respect of a schoolboy before the despotic glance of his teacher.

The maestro took a dark handkerchief from the pocket of his trousers and laid it down on the lectern, he lightly brushed the keyboard with two fingers, coughed once again and kept staying still. The moment preceding the beginning kept me in suspense: the pianist lifted both hands, kept them suspended over the keyboard in search of concentration, then he dropped them with affected heaviness.

And the sounds came out of the piano as invoked by the will of a wizard.

The heaviness of the first notes produced in me the effect of a sudden awakening, the exit from a hypnotic condition which had estranged me from the context. I recognized the incipit of Mozart's Fantasia in C minor.

I was captured by the not unfamiliar feeling of annihilation, of disaggregation of the spirit induced by the witchcraft of the sounds. In those moments I has the sharp sensation that I did not belong to me, as if I were awakened from a centennial sleep and being launched into a time that was not my own: "that" time did not belong to me, "that" space did not belong to me. It seemed as if I had been granted the privilege, and the fatigue, to watch over future but known events being conscious, however, that I could not modify their course according to my desire.

Usually this state of mind drove me to daydream about how different could have been the course of my existence if a tricky spirit, still without a name, had not made his best to turn upside down the series of events that, at least in my imagination, should have lead me there, on the scene.

I admit that, when I still was a student, imagination was my fuel, and thinking of "sacrificing life on the altar of art" elated me. There was only a little insignificant particular: it all was just an ideal construction which left behind the reality and the control of the analysis, a magnificent set and a perfect script in which I was the interpreter of a role decidedly out of my reach.

This is the witchcraft that entrapped me, and it took a long, painful time to realize a partial truth: I had ambition and desire, the desire fed the illusion, the illusion made a sensational division between reality and imagination. The circuit kept going on and on, until . . .

It was the year '77, the venue Pescara: national contest of pianistic performance.

I played in a duo with a fellow companion. Between us there was not a strong feeling: we met each other only few times during that summer because we lived in two different cities. Nevertheless we had just performed the end of term show, held in may in the big hall of the conservatoire. We did our best, receiving applauses and flattening congratulations. The teacher of History sat not far from my piano, and with the blink of my eye I could see on his face an expression of satisfaction and joy.

But in august, in Pescara, things were different.

The two grand pianos set one in front of the other created between us a distance that seemed even bigger than the distance between our cities. They seemed long enough to frighten us. And then there was a jury. A jury! They took it very seriously. It was no longer an audience of relatives, fellows and some teacher you did not need to feel scared of.

Three people in an engrossed mood were sitting near the footrest where the pianos stayed. Two men and a woman. One of them seemed to be there by mistake, because he looked more interested in thinking about his own vicissitudes: he kept on moving, trembling while shaking nervously on the chair. Maybe he was a famous performer, but he looked rather like a boor with a slight bohemian nuance.

Definitely a jury, damn it!

I wonder what those three were thinking about: would they find two competitors of agreeable appearance? What about that arrogant little beard? And what about those jeans? Would everything be in harmony with their mood? Because there was no hope that their mood would not interfere in their final decision.

So, we were one in front of the other, my fellow and I, separated by a cosmic distance. Between us an invisible wall, and our worried glances would be of no use, so would the attempts to communicate with a movement of the body. I felt as a dreamer who opens his mouth to scream in a desperate need of help, and instead is not able to give breath. There was no time for suggestions, for exchanging recommendations, and very little had been the time to recover a feeling that the distance and the time had partially broken. My fellow seemed a stranger to me, an irresponsible who did not care whether the attacks coincided, whether the tempo was abruptly increasing or decreasing, even if everything was, I would rather say, going to hell. It seemed that he did not notice anything, or rather wisely he preferred to ignore that, just because it was impossible to return back in the time. And as if it were not enough . . . what's up . . . my hand, shit! My right hand does not work . . . I feel as if someone pulled me! What is pulling me? My hand seems wanting to get away from the keyboard just while that passage is arriving: yes I know, I've done it incorrectly seven times out of ten, but this time I have to make it right, the passage with the right hand must come out well, Christ! But who is it . . . what is pulling me?

I could not imagine it at that time, but there was a will—I do not know how to describe it in another way—a crawling and stubborn will that had chosen my body, my

15

right arm, to assert itself. It was nesting into my muscles, into my tendons, my articulations, and did not seem intentioned to let go. I was granting to this will a physical consistency but I could not give it a face or a name. I felt it as mighty as invisible.

That circumstance was the first deep snatch in the plot of self deceptions that had sustained me till then. It was just like watching a picture in which a pleasant landscape obliged me to do a difficult operation: to gaze at the landscape, to observe it from far, to concentrate on the snatch and capture the essence of the optical illusion. What I perceived of myself could be demolished in a moment, if I only gazed at the snatch.

I could not suspect that I should start from there, from that symptom, the joke of a devil, who was not ready to barter his power with anything else. He did not ask my soul in exchange for glory, but he obliged me to suffer and satisfy every and each of his desires. It simply and tragically was the surrender, the defeat, because that was his will, a unilateral renunciation.

I would have fought, of course, trying to resist and to keep the scaffolding of illusion and the supports of the remainder of my will. It was so cruel asking me to give up that image of myself I laboriously had created, to give up that future full of triumphs for me.

During the course of time I developed a painful incapacity to articulate my fingers. Muscles, tendons and the articulation of the wrist almost got to paralysis. My right arm became a stranger to me, a separated, dead part, with a hostile autonomous will.

The occasional jovial person politely remarked that I could be satisfied with "simply" playing the piano, giving up the idea of the "top". "Basically", they said, "the most important thing is to reach acceptable technical levels". Those distributors of wise pieces of advice could not imagine the fracture between a redundant feeling absolutely unwilling to compromise and the limits deriving from a part of the self completely and inflexibly gone mad. Facing superhuman pressures, the reason could only consider escaping from itself as a solution.

The roar of a noisy waterfall took me back in the hall. Mozart's Fantasia was finished and the pianist was smiling while taking a bow with affected superiority.

He almost noticed me while turning towards my side, and I had to pull away. Doing that, I crushed against the wall behind, and the surprise hammered into my skin causing a sharp pain in my kidney. The pain took me back to the intention that had brought me there: the concert, of course, my old fellow come back, sure . . . I felt hinted down. I rested my hand on the rigid form by my side as if I tried to gather and hold my intentions.

Again the pianist's shoulders, his torso slightly bending over the keyboard, his head lifted and, I could imagine, his glance towards a certain point in the empty space, waiting for a click to activate in his mind in a few moments.

He began the "Pathetica" and the heavy minor chord violently impressed into my stomach. After all, the relation between music and my body remained a mystery to me, far beyond the obvious connection in using the body parts for playing an instrument. Say I could not catch the "mystic value" of it.

The fact is that an idea, the attempt of interpretation rising up from my mind, used to live separately from the instrument that should render it musically. Having necessarily to pass through the matter, the body, it seemed that the idea got polluted and vulgar during this journey from conception to realization, losing its original energy into the filaments of the body, resulting in a distorted, faded, almost unrecognizable copy of the original idea.

From my point of observation the gestures of the pianist let me think of a trained monkey carrying out its exercises with commitment. I was staring at that back as if trying to penetrate and hide myself into it just to feel the consistence of its blood, the quality of the air circulating in his lungs, of his heart, what kind of matter his brain was made of, what was the form of his intelligence.

One evening, a Russian pianist unexpectedly dropped into our class room at the conservatoire. There were six of us having a break between our lessons. Our teacher, very young and a prodigy in a way, had gone outside the room for a coffee and, as it often happened in similar situations, we were having fun playing the two pianos in turn.

Jazz mixed with fragments of fashionable songs. Who sat at a piano was immediately and abruptly evicted. So Bach had to stay silent because Chopin had just been called back in life by other hands. On the other piano the protagonist was Clementi, whose "Gradus" was getting angry an eight-teen years old very pretty girl, who attended the eight course—"Listen, why don't we see each other, we could set up a duo, what do you think?"

Suddenly the room appeared to have been always silent and empty when a discreet and timorous man came in. None of us had ever met him personally, but we all immediately recognized him, for we had seen many times his photos on the covers of the records. A real myth, at least for us, had entered the room creating a real effect of alienation.

We looked at each other questioning, unable to express anything. Besides, we could not communicate with the living myth, because we did not know a single word of Russian, and he did not speak Italian.

The Russian took seat at the piano and remained still: we all thought that he was obviously looking for concentration. Actually, we did not really understand what was going on, as that search for concentration prolonged far beyond the limits of an embarrassed waiting.

The living myth was going to perform in a concert in our town the next day. He had come to the conservatoire to practice, and evidently he did not appreciate our presence on his mythical way.

It became evident when, after a while, the Russian heavily sat on the stool (he was tall and stout). He mechanically rubbed his hands and kept turning the pages of the score looking for something. We six could not make a decision: we should leave the room, but we were quite disappointed because we were already determined to attend to that unscheduled lesson, a master in piano, and we were perfectly sure that such an opportunity would not occur a second time.

The big man at the piano, his shoulders rather similar to those of a woodcutter, was indifferent to all that. He just kept on motionless, waiting for us to definitely leave the room.

We had to make a decision!

After a short and confused negotiation we tried to tell the living myth that we would have considered an incomparable privilege the opportunity to attend his performance, even if only for a few minutes. The maestro smiled benevolently and spoke, in French, by means of his secretary-interpreter, a young man, terribly tall and skinny, who had followed the maestro immediately after. "The maestro grants to you no more than ten minutes".

We almost reached the ecstasy.

He started with a sonata by Prokofiev, and began with a wrong note that aroused amazement and a little laugh: wow, even myths make mistakes, I thought. The maestro repeated the initial passage more than once and, when he finally had removed the dust off the keyboard with an arpeggio from the sharp to the grave notes researching the correct sonority and the necessary muscular weight, he abruptly stopped and remained inexplicably still.

It was his manner to let us understand it was now time to leave him alone. Right, he had satisfied us showing how the big ones work, and we even enjoyed a wrong note live—even myths make mistakes—now out!

In that classroom, in that circumstance, observing the sturdy, woodcutter's back of the Russian myth, I for the first time happened to think that something special had to lie in the fiber of his body, a sort of biological intelligence inside his tendons, his muscles, his articulations, an abstract substance, a will organizing the infinite contractions and excitements of the flesh, which otherwise would have be contorted, would have tripped in itself without any purpose, without the opportunity to determine significant events, like carrying out a performance.

Reluctantly, of course, we slowly paraded out of the room, shaking hands with him in an almost religious respect, as if he were a relic. Ah, how easily people express admiration for the artist committed in noble causes, look at him as the chosen one, a pure untainted soul, preferring to ignore that, as I happened to hear, "he too possesses an ass hole".

In a while the first part of the concert would be over, since they were playing the Rondo. I kept turning on my stall and could not stop tormenting the bulge at my side with my left hand. The continuous friction was producing heat, a sensation that melted with the humidity of the sweat dripping down from the armpit. I could feel in the hall a tension going to ease in an applause; the pianist was bent on the keyboard, slightly on the right, and caressed the keys preparing to the last descending arpeggio.

The last cadence, the mighty chords of the left hand, the sonata was over. He triumphantly lifted his hands from the keyboard and waited for the applause. A lady in the first row was frantically agitating her small and stocky hands and smiled satisfied, turning glancing from the right to the left and shaking her head. From my place I could see only her. The audience's delirium, on the contrary, reached me with a rumble that resounded just when the pianist kept his hands away from the keyboard.

The pianist took some bows, with his left hand leant against the piano and his right hand blatantly on his heart. The man with the task of turning the pages was the only one to remain on his place, while the rest of the audience was caught by a tremendous and almost indecent exaltation.

Lights ran over the hall and almost abruptly composure replaced the agitation of the ladies and gentlemen in dark suit, the no-man's-land determined by the half-light returned to be delimited by the borders of appearance: the turning on of the lights meant as well the turning on of appropriateness and social hierarchies.

The rendez-vous was at the bar inside the theatre, which slowly became crowded when the hall got empty. This ceremony of the ceremonies would obscure the concert and its protagonist with frivolous pleasantries and unsuspected comments. That is why I remained behind my barricade. I detested worldliness, even the small provincial one, because I knew that for most of those people what really mattered was being there, meet again to restore and strengthen social bonds of caste. As for myself, I always avoided crowded places, the masses without character and, above all, the evenings like this. I was there but would rather not be there, I was there tenaciously resisting the thought of becoming like the rest of them.

I looked at them, sometimes, with a piercing sensation, I weighed them with a seemingly unprovoked sarcasm, actually suggested by bulky feelings of superiority, or inferiority perhaps, bulky because unresolved. From my dark hiding place I heard the voices coming from the corridor, the shrill voice of a woman commenting the pianist's performance raised up through the indistinct murmuring. She said: "He has grown enormously up since the last time I heard him, do you remember? It was shortly before he left for Salzburg. Tonight's Mozart is light years away from those days' Mozart, moreover ten years have passed. The technique is still amazing, like then! It 'always been his strong point since he was a student . . . do you agree?"

I caught only a few incomplete sentences of a baritone voice: " . . . I am puzzled, I do not know . . . the technique is . . . right . . . leaves a profound doubt . . . superficial . . . completely convincing."

I had to admit that between his views and mine there was an unexpected affinity. The doubts that man expressed had been the same I had since the time of the conservatory, when they had raised in me a cautious distrust with respect to his "artistic maturity", doubts that still remained, except for the robustness of the technique, that could not be in discussion. In fact, envy was plotting even then, although in the dark. But the distrust in my companion had a background character, say ideological, and it was the expression of a different approach to the piano: exasperated and magmatic was mine, balanced and more aware was his. In a word, the Dionysian and the Apollonian. These differences, exalted in the comparison, made me doubt of his actual value, in the sense of "yes, the technique is important, but the sensitivity, the musicality . . ."

The fact that I was hiding while my mate was there on stage, was the paradoxical demonstration of how I was wrong: I should have prepared the way to the magma before allowing it to spread, but if this has already happened, it is difficult, if not impossible, to get to control it . . .

The room was getting crowded again, the buzz was growing thicker.

This time the man who's task was turning the pages preceded the pianist, from my seat I could see him well: short gray hair, a bristly still black mustache, he had a melancholy expression, staring as if hypnotized at a point in the empty space. He was short, he had both his feet resting placidly on the boards of the stage and from the whole of his person emanated a sense of rigid asceticism. Were it not for the slight and rapid pattering of his fingers on the score on his knees, one would consider him as a piece of furniture or a scenic element.

Unexpectedly, he moved and looked in my direction, it was a quick movement of the head, top right, for a moment our eyes met and I had no time to draw back to avoid it. A member of the audience seated in that dais should appear rather natural to him, but still he could not help but show a certain disappointment, he wrinkled for a moment his eyebrows, he slightly shook his shoulders and returned to contemplate the empty space.

Lights were turned down again, and the grip in my stomach, that had lasted during all the interval, finally disappeared.

The pianist reappeared, repeating his ritual: bow, stool, handkerchief in his hands. The other man put on the lectern the score of the Sonata in B minor with terrible slowness. I could read the title page.

Hidden in my bunker, I was beginning to wonder when I should carry out the surprise for my companion, whether during the performance, perhaps taking advantage of one of those spectacular moments of sound scattered along the sonata, or at the end of his performance, when the pianist would bow to his audience, to his fellow citizens to gather the unconditional consent, one could imagine, they would not have denied to him: in my indecision, I let myself be seduced by Liszt. Liszt's music had the power to exalt me, but that night it seemed to act on me like a quick effect sedative, I began to contemplate my autonomic nervous system.

The darkness produced in me a reassuring effect of containment, it was not necessary to beware of the insistent curiosity, inevitable in a confined situation like that. My hands were stretched out, resting on my thighs, I took the liberty to adhere softly to my seat and I felt a delicate general wellness. I crossed my legs and rested my elbows on the parapet, I no longer felt the weight on my side, no hassle, I mentally followed the contours of it as if it were a natural protuberance of my body. I stopped sweating profusely and the painful contractions of my groin had given way to a pleasant tingle.

It was time to become familiar with the surprise.

When I had pulled it out of a locked drawer it immediately seemed to me a foreign, useless, even hostile object, a stupid piece of metal with a thin and elongated shape, but elegant, in its way a work of art. Now I lingered with it in my hands, not daring to look at it. I no longer remembered when or where or why I bought it, a luxurious expense, a beautiful object to hold and to look at, nothing more. Besides pursuing this criterion I had bought paintings, records, books, and all manner of useless objects. I wonder if, when I bought it, I was not already following a hidden and still confused plan, a premonition or destiny, maybe nothing happens by chance and the sense of things, or at least a very minor part of it, is painfully revealed to us years later, while, when they happen, they seem to follow the logic of whim. The paralysis in my right arm seemed to me one of these incomprehensible, capricious events, that time would reveal together with an inescapable truth: I would never become a concert pianist, and the incomprehensibility of that symptom should have appeared to me as a clear premonition: "Be careful, do not challenge the limits that should remain impassable, stop your mind . . . or your arms."

Now I knew that, so I would not stop my hand. I certainly could not hope to get away with it, everyone would hear the shots and the direction from which they came, the pianist would blatantly collapse, perhaps hit to death. I was there just for that. It was my way to ransom from a dull existence, from destiny, from necessity, from logic and common sense, it would be my irreverence to the imponderable and the nonsense of existence. I had lost my bet with life, but I wanted to show that I did not care about "the need to give up", easy for all the occasional wise advisers, and among them also my analyst—yes, because there has been one.

I do not want to bore you with further recriminations, I only say that I am currently in jail, waiting for the trial. I can tell you that I do not repent, that I have no moral weight, it makes no sense speaking about moral. Is life moral? And is defeat? And is failure moral? Puah . . .

Oh, I almost forgot to tell you when I did it. Well! At the end, during the applauses. A bullet pierced his neck, another one tucked into his right temple, death was almost instantaneous, but he had time enough for enjoying his triumph: he still had a smile on his lips when they picked him up.

Humoresque

· · · · · · · · · · · · · · · · · ·

(fragments of a spring day)

Fragment 1

THAT MORNING THE ALARM DID not ring. He had just opened his eyes, and before raising from bed he waited for the bell tolls spread by a loudspeaker located on the dome of a church not far from his house. Then he realized he was late, that morning he had missed the strokes that, in sync with the alarm, announced it was 7.00 A.M.

He could remember that he had dreamed. He was a pianist, a virtuoso, and created a series of harmonies that vaguely recalled Mozart; he maneuvered the keys, he covered the keyboard with his right hand especially, weaving bel canto style arabesques, while his left hand, almost motionless, seemed to scan time with chords that supported the airy part of his right hand.

He remained laying down, while the images of the dream kept him busy. A sense of well-being made him feel vaguely floating, fantasies and thoughts floating in a fluid with no ties.

When he finally decided to jump off the bed, he lifted the covers with a quick movement and a night time humor smell instantly dissolved like a cloud of steam. He sat up, looked around disappointed, prey of a subtle and indefinable bad mood.

Since long he had obliged himself to a forced isolation. "To set his ideas in order", he repeated to himself and to those among the people around him who asked about his strange behavior. In that late March morning, not quite spring, rather mildly winter, he felt that it was time to break the barrier he had raised between himself and the world. He thought that he would like to visit his friend Oscar. By a curious and inexplicable association, he remembered a picture stack on the wall of Oscar's room, which showed the resigned, suffering face of an old and wrinkled man contracted in the grimace preceding the cry, which seemed to keep the thoughts that would soon materialize in two streams of tears.

From the window the view opened on a dark green mass that laid at the feet of the building and disappeared into a near horizon, a boundary marked by a row of close houses forming a barrier to the green of the park. He slowly pulled the strap of the shutter with regular movements, and the light of that lazy March day sneaked into the room. He felt the rain intermittently pattering on the floor of the terrace, gathering in a hive and disappearing beneath, along the sidewalk. He stood behind the glass of the window admiring the arabesques of rain droplets embroidered on the external surface.

They fell as if shot by an invisible hand and disintegrated, while only a small amount of water would stick to the smooth surface of the glass. With the impact, some sister-droplets merged together, still following the path that seemed assigned to them and then they plunged, heavier, down in the abyss, not without leaving behind them an invisible trace.

Over the parapet of the terrace he began to focus on the long and straight street. The show was that of an endless theory of poles, benches and trees, still bald and sad, on one side; on the other side, well-kept flower beds whose geometric disposition, orderly and predictable, made them insignificant to his eyes. Below, timeless, cars and umbrellas dotted the background of this "Landscape in the rain." Reluctantly he pulled away from the scene and moved toward the bathroom, dragging a pair of old red slippers. He could well say that those deformed slippers had bore for months the weight of his long and bony body, patient as companions whose loyalty was guarantee of security and continuity.

In vain he would seek elsewhere allies willing to drag along with his body also the burden of thoughts. And what about his pajamas, every night forced to take unnatural positions to meekly support the folds and contours of his body.

Had it not been for them, and for his friendly books, that voluntary exile would have solved in a hard and senseless imprisonment.

In the short distance separating the window from the bathroom door he passed his hand in his hair, as if wanting to ensure that together with it, still there were his thoughts, his intentions and the ghosts that animated them: yes, he was there with his hair and everything else.

In the tiny space of the bathroom, a stench of stale and of urine grew stagnant; he stood in front of the cup and began to rummage into his groin. That sour smell seemed to move ancient moods, to awaken wild instincts sleeping under piles of rules and prohibitions, insidious superstructures that destroyed, under the guise of civilized life, the inescapable and grinning bestiality.

He pointed his flaccid and wrinkled penis toward the mouth of the cup and waited for the contractions of the abdomen, to which delicately counterpointed liquid sensations that the slow and gradual emptying of the bladder gave him. He moved to the left, turned the knob of hot water and waited; he washed his hands and face with soap, he put a cotton stick in his ear, and rummaged through his armpits.

Before closing the door he saw his fleeting reflection in the oval glass on the wall to the left and thought he needed to stop and scan the picture—oh, how many times he had granted this need to arise, and how many times he had supported it almost like a pagan ceremony officiated on the altar of his own narcissism, and yet that morning he thought it unnecessary.

The door handle was frozen. He went out on the landing as one who verifies with relief—and a slight euphoria that is communicated to the groin—that he basically had feared for nothing.

Fragment 2

HE REMEMBERED THAT THE SKY was dark, but glaring cracks created and the uniform surface appeared to tear in several points and left the blue filter through.

He thought: If I could immerse myself in a bath of joy. Far, far from certain routes of the mind that, like labyrinths, seem to leave little chance to a harmonic and balanced motion . . . What prevents me from seeing the announcing spring? Far . . .

A bath of cheerfulness and maybe I would see the colors, smell the perfumes, chase the pollens . . . Far.

A voice from inside pressed him mercilessly: but spring is an invention of the poets, an idea brought forth in the grip of turmoil hormonal disturbances, it is just a page out of an anthology.

He stopped listening to it and surrendered to a thought that seemed incongruous but soothing: there is a season to be born and one to die, one to cry and one to smile, one for pain and another to recover and heal . . . Well, perhaps spring is a new idea, he thought, and he recalled the verses of an unknown poet:

> . . . The thoughts, the movements
> tune their instruments
> of poignant timbre
> with the forms that are reborn
> animated by the same breath

and the voice of time
sings a new song.

He would call Oscar.

He slipped into a phone box—a rare one by now, but he hated the cellular phone—and dialed the number. He waited for the voice from the other end.

"Hello!"

"Hello . . . Could I talk to Oscar?"

He knew that voice, it was his father. Despite a massif size and a stocky and sharp face, unusually tanned, he displayed a disarming shyness.

"Let me call him for you."

The voice faded, but he remained glued to the receiver waiting for the thinning out of the rough and shy sweetness of that voice.

He thought that in no case would that man enter his life, but he was in his thoughts now, and he had to admit that he could not—he had never been able, in fact—define the shifting contours, the nuances that melt on the canvas as a representation of love.

"Hello, tell me."

"I'd like to see you, would you?"

"Okay, tell me when."

"I was thinking about tonight."

"I'll wait for you."

He left the phone box and walked towards a destination he still ignored. The sky showed larger breaks, the grey mantle was gradually but inexorably swept by a violent wind.

Fragment 3

THE PATH HE TOOK LED him invariably to the places he loved to travel along when he was invaded by ancient recalls.

There was a tree-lined avenue, which turned in a slight curve, and a road cutting perpendicularly, and, in front of him, three possibilities. He knew that choosing one would mean entering into a sort of dimension of no return, that makes us look at the streets, at the people and at the thoughts behind us as objects now lost forever. He chose the avenue.

He went from one tree to another, he touched the trunks, and the gesture seemed to put him in communion with the living material of which they were made, it was as if a fluid swarmed from them and rested on everything around. He went through an old porch, whose stones were blackened by time and dirt, and through the porch he seemed to enter a dimension that had the charm of things put away and forgotten. That was the entrance to the village. The houses, the shop windows on the sides of the streets.

One house in particular attracted him, a Pompeian red façade with windows and balconies, which was several centuries old. Property of an old aristocratic family, which included a patriot, an anarchist and generous to the cause: his wealth squandered, and also his spirit had dissolved. The perfect stone edges seemed to cut the air through.

A little further there was a church of rigorous plant. S.Giacomo's looked like a stretched body, wistfully thinking back to the past: he perceived it as a projection of his mind. He loved that church, and the tower of the sundial, now useless, that had become nothing more than an old church to the eye of the passerby. He wrapped it in a tender embrace and caressed it with his eyes, careful not to wake it from the sleep in which it had fallen since the local residents had stopped considering it an eleventh century church, to think of her just as "old S.Giacomo's".

He reluctantly pulled away and turned left. He took an unclean driveway, full of smells that he recognized as those of his childhood. A sharp breeze crept in the unreal silence, almost unknown to the city's big boulevards.

In fact he saw the silence, behind the half-closed door of an old one-floor house, in the silent and questioning glance of an old woman who hid when she saw him there, probably wondering who was that intruder who dared to violate the silence with the thump of his paces and his indiscreet eyes. He would talk to her, tell her that he was there just for that silence, that she had nothing to fear, that he was looking just for a sound that could give new voice to silence. "Come out from your stony hiding place", he wanted to tell her, "I recognize you, I recognize your features, gestures, intentions tasting of melancholy. Do not be scared, and wrap me with your blanket of wool, as soft as silk."

The road was marked by a double row of doors and windows stained with green and brown, interrupted at regular intervals by very brief and clear rough stone steps, which connected the inner part of the houses to the dirty paving. Balconies and windows were made heavier by rows of clothes hanging to dry. The laundry shook, uniting its voice to the breeze rising from the sea and creeping in the alleys.

The occasional people who walked along the lanes had an expression of resentment, they looked down and paced fast.

At a turn he found himself in front of an irregularly shaped square, occupied by a multitude of colorful and bustling market stalls. The fish sellers shook, surrounded by pools of black water that smelled of sea, the butcher's stalls looks like puppet theaters fascinating and contending the buyers. People packed into double and triple rows to witness the spectacle of the fruit crates reflecting the sunlight.

He immersed himself in that menagerie, and as he gradually got lost among those people, he felt as being on a stage whose backdrop consisted of a colorful row of three-storey houses beat by the sunlight. The crisp air and the odors emitted from the stalls, seemed to excite that shapeless mass. The façades on the backdrop seemed to laugh at them.

He reached a fishmonger's stall and got fascinated by the orderly arrangement of boxes full of colorful fish. Wet and perfumed, they were full of shining shrimps, anchovies with lost eyes, while mullets were standing in line, stocky, faded and still gasping. A little farther, black stained cuttlefish, abandoned on the bottom as exhausted and deflated ectoplasms. A pile of mussels, collected in plaits and placed one on the other, was waiting to be separated. In the middle of the stall, in the place of honor, stood out the superb, large mullets, of a silvery gray with pale shades of blue, and an old resentment on their muzzles. And then a multitude of other occupants of the deep abysses, with their strange shapes and their unpronounceable names.

"How much for the prawns", a woman asked the fishmonger, who seemed to dominate her from behind the stall. She accompanied the question with a grimace of disgust.

She accompanied the request with a grimace of disgust, as one who is going to refuse, even before knowing the answer, and will move away indignant about the greediness of the request.

"Twelve."

The lady turned on her heels and walked away muttering, putting on her disappointment: that fish was not worth that money.

Fragment 4

HE HAD JUST LEFT A bar, where he had ordered a coffee with a dash of milk.

Taking coffee with milk was a habit he had passively contracted during an August afternoon, many years before.

At that time he was madly in love with a busty eighteen year old girl, an explosive blonde of whom he knew by heart the essential body parts. He had joined her at a seaside resort in the South, where he spent the holiday as a guest of some of his relatives from Florence. One dull afternoon he heard a guy—someone who could claim a theoretical and potentially reversible link with the girl—who was speaking peremptorily to her, as she poured a steaming coffee, asking to add "milk, please."

He was as well a blond teenager, and he envied his beauty, his apparent self-confidence, and he attributed to him a charm that he felt he did not possess . . .

Just turning a corner, he came to the bus station, a place frequented very little. What attracted him of that place were the remains of an ancient unraveled church, of which a side aisle had survived, with the bells and pillars still visible, some mullioned windows and an apse ridiculously protected by a railing: the bus terminal was in the place where once there must have been the side altars.

He leaned against a pole and remained observing those remains, around him the buzzing of mute and faceless silhouettes, long coats, hats, useless umbrellas. He did not know whether the din around him was cause or effect of the other one inside. Yet he felt prisoner of a thought, despite the apparent freedom that the circular chaos promised. He was motionless, leaning against the pole, and thought about death.

Trying to imagine where the soul would run away from was a complex exercise, given that it would have the tenacity to endure till the end and not, on the contrary, be prematurely worn little by little, filament by filament, puff by puff, strain after strain; and maybe at the end just a faint sigh would remain, the proverbial exhalation, what remained of an account opened and dried up years before, without much trumpet blast, he thought. And then what? A peremptory voice called his name.

"Umberto!"

That voice went through and shook him violently, he turned with a jolt. In front of him an old woman in a brown coat, gray hair hung down behind her ears, an indecipherable expression written on her face. He recognized her face with difficulty, he recalled it to memory as younger, healthier, and free from the androgynous hair that covered her chin. She was a dear, old family friend, like a second mother to him.

The sight of the woman confused him, as if a past time he believed dead resurfaced unexpectedly. As if swiftly making out a secret area, a shelter that consciousness explores with difficulty, for fear of moving heavy boulders.

He watched the old woman, her gray hair, her wrinkles, the coat that wrapped a shapeless form, and he tried by all means to deny that what was in front of him was just a sham of the young, energetic, imperious, dark haired woman he remembered. She used to show a pride that intimidated him, and now there remained only a ghost.

He wanted to hug her, and yet he remained motionless. He reached out his hand and offered a warm handshake: at least the contact would surrogate the unsaid.

"How are you? How many years since you went away from home . . . You know, I wasn't able to come to see you . . ."

She paused, as if the words she had just uttered put her in front of an intimate contradiction.

"The truth is that . . . I was afraid, yes, that's it. I am old now, I have seen other times, I know fears that no one knows. I felt unable to accept your decision to leave the house, slamming the door . . . In fact I did not want you to feel my embarrassment, to interpret it as a refusal . . . I had to accept it, if you had decided so, it was your life . . . It was right that you followed your way."

The past time which for years had lived in a hermetically sealed room, seemed to have decided to show itself, to be recognized. It was there in front of him, it was that woman who was afraid of having to apologize for nothing.

While she talked, he wondered whether it made sense to speak of past and present, since time seemed to have stopped and past and present were mixed. Dividing time into fragments with the sole purpose of enabling us to recall in our mind what we were, what we are and what we will be, appeared to him a vain exercise.

The woman kept on talking, he stared at her without listening, just following the thread of his thoughts.

Time seemed to him rather motionless, immutable, without a beginning and without an end, an idea continually resurgent, perceptible by observing the face of a child, the calm movements of a man, those uncertain of an old man with his stick, grabbing to it as he grabbed to all the illusions he had to forget, and to all the steps he had to make to keep together the moments of existence that time granted him. This is time, he thought. Child, young, old, always different and always the same.

"Well, here comes my bus, I have to go . . . And do not think about all the nonsense that I've told you . . . you know, I am an old man, now."

Fragment 5

THERE WAS A PLATE: "CHORAL J. S. BACH. He entered.

He didn't know that part of the city, the 167 zone. The room was enlightened by windows located at the top. There were three rows of benches and a platform at the bottom. He looked around and sat down on the last pew on the right. He was alone in the room, while the platform was crowding up. When the director arrived, immediately the hum coming from the dais stopped. He greeted, looked right and left and sat on a chair in front of the choir. He said something, then he concentrated on the score.

Latecomers arrived when the teacher was giving instructions. He was a stocky priest, with long black hair on his neck, his fat hands were as white as his shirt collar. He could see him well under the cone of neon light that dominated him, and his hands, he thought, where more accustomed to handle scores than the sacred ornaments.

The teacher started a phrase and a song expanded into the hall, joined him and got him excited. He thought he recognized a passage from Vivaldi's "Gloria". He stood up and decided to come nearer.

From the place he was now occupying, a few meters from the sopranos, he thought he recognized a face, and when their eyes met he smiled uncertainly. It was just her. That woman, like others, had prompted his fantastic universe, long ago. He had met her at some friends', and the glacial folds of her lips and her sharp eyes had fascinated him. It took little to trigger what he called "the syndrome of indifference." It was always like that, every time: indifference, in a woman, weakened him, forcing him to cover, in strict and predictable ascent, a range of moods, from disguised attention to cautious interest, to the push to move towards the woman, to disillusionment, to melancholic resignation. It was not the physical distance, was the other one, that makes separate worlds out of a man and a woman, sometimes clashing. It was that movement into a no man's land of uncertain boundaries, which sometimes a gesture or a look authorize to cover.

The teacher stopped the execution, he talked long, he explained, moving his hands, he signaled the breaths, smiled and asked the tenors to repeat.

He tried to speak to the girl but he stopped in time, he simply made a gesture, that she returned.

They found each other in the street at the end of the rehearsal.

"I have a car, shall we go?"

"Let's go!"

They headed towards the sea, the girl's gaze was fixed on the road and protected by a pair of dark glasses that made her enigmatic. He hated sunglasses, and sometimes also those who wore them. They turned into an avenue leading to the beach.

To escape the anxiety and avoid thinking he fixed his attention on a big dog who preceded them in the back of a van.

"Where have you been all this time?"

"Nowhere."

"Those friends, have you seen them again?"

"Occasionally."

"How come I haven't heard of you anymore, why you haven't looked for me anymore?"

"I do not know, but you know . . ."

"Yes?"

"Do not smile, please, what I'm about to say will seem silly . . ."

"Well?"

"You made me curious and worried . . . Why are you smiling? I was right thinking that I would say something silly."

"No, not at all. I always do this effect."

They kept silent. The van with the dog was left behind.

"What are you thinking about?"

"Nothing."

The car ran. They took a driveway lined with huge chestnut trees. In the background he saw a thin bright blue streak. The half-deserted road encouraged high speed, behind the city faded and the brilliant streak invaded the background, the sun went down.

The car slowed and finally stopped near a kiosk that was closed. A slight breeze stirred the oleanders lining the sidewalk. They got out and directed to the battle, he was slightly behind her. His eyes traveled along her body.

They stopped a few steps from the sea, in silence, staring at the slightly rippled surface.

"How is going the work at the Academy?"

"Nothing special."

"Do you often come to the sea?"

"When I need to think, sometimes."

"Do you come here alone?"

"Yes. I sit and I listen to the silence, to the sea."

"And what do you think about?"

"Oh, about so many things and nothing in particular. The sea helps me to feel nostalgia."

"Really? It is funny."

"Not really. When I feel the nostalgia coming, I know something is leaving me."

The girl looked away, staring at a point on the horizon. They were close, he could smell her perfume, perceive the girl's breath. She said: "Go ahead."

"I say farewell to old thoughts, to images of people that maybe I'll never see again, to scraps of dreams. I make room to the regret for those feelings that were not able to express themselves. I talk to the sea and it answers me."

"Does it talk? And of what?"

"Of its boundless solitude. It tells of what it hides and preserves, of what he takes from men and of what it returns. It's as if it abandoned its words on the beach when this is empty. It talks . . . it talks and never stops."

They remained silent for long, staring at the sea.

Fragment 6

OSCAR'S HOUSE WAS FULL OF piled up smells. Sometimes it seemed like a grocery store, of those impossible to find, by now. Four people lived there: his father and mother, his sister, and Oscar. Very discreet people, they moved from a room to another as shadows. He knew well Oscar's house, he had to cross the entire town to reach it. Invariably, the pilgrimage to Oscar's ended in the arms of a large armchair, always the same, lined with a sad cloth. He had learned to know Oscar, his smile, his looks and his discomforts day by day, since they had known for years.

Usually, music served as a prologue to the evening that they would spend together, the last hours of the day waited to be spent.

Oscar had received him as usual, and as usual it seemed to him to enter a world that, despite everything, still escaped from him. They sat side by side, Oscar had a book in his hands.

"What are you reading?"

Oscar stood up to turn down the volume, they were listening to a concert for piano and orchestra by Mozart, the KV 415.

"A collection of letters. Two writers who have never met personally. They exchanged critics and suggestions, they esteemed each other. Their epistolary friendship was irretrievably broken when one of them published a novel that the other considered immoral, ordering, "for Heaven's sake ", to delete some parts of the book. The author was gay, the other fellow was Catholic: he deplored the tendencies of the other and begged him to "redeem", but the other obviously did not listen to him."

"What happened in the end?"

"They stopped writing to each other."

"And the letters?"

"There was someone who took the trouble to collect and preserve them, a fanatical collector. He gathered them and then sold them for a very large sum."

They stopped talking, the music took ownership of silence, the Rondo was spinning towards the fanciful conclusion.

He said: "Let me accompany you tonight. Will you not?"

He had often wondered, what could push someone like Oscar to endure a ritual that was humiliating. He did not disapprove Oscar, nor he had a moralistic attitude towards his choices, he simply wanted to understand, and for him to understand meant to be there, to live a situation from within, to understand its meaning.

Oscar consented, amused and embarrassed by the unusual request.

He would accompany Oscar in his evening stroll, he would follow him at a distance, spy on him with discretion. He would live the adventure of stalking, of coming and going, of the signals. He would mix with the humanity that every night crowded the waiting room of a station, or a dark sidewalk; he would listen, hidden in a cramped and smelly toilet, to noises, to the voices of that clandestine trade of delusions.

The fracture he perceived when he tried to arrange the opposites in Oscar's life, escaped to his ability of reconciliation;

during the day, he was a respected and competent public servant; by night, he was a ghost forced to beg company, to get lost into the shadows of unknown frequenters of dark and out of the way cinemas, rancid places full of accomplice and lascivious whispers, of furtive movements, which encouraged a fugitive and desperate sex.

"Why?"

"Just curiosity."

They went out together as agreed, it was dark outside. The street below the house was jammed with cars and pedestrians, some people lingered at the crossroad, mostly young men. Oscar didn't pass up the opportunity to observe some of them closely. He was embarrassed, but anyway no one ordered him to follow his friend: the game was about to start, and he decided to play, he could not avoid the rules.

"Where are we going?"

"To the cinema 'Odeon', you know?"

"The one near the port?"

"Exactly."

"Will we enter?"

"Only for a while. There is much movement, good fishing."

Oscar took off the pale mask of the employee, to assume the role of the frivolous, worldly, intriguing and a bit pathetic man, master of the mechanisms of approaching. He was well dressed, perfumed, he sang an aria from *La Traviata*. Out of the breast pocket of his jacket, an eye-catching bright red scarf could be seen, clashing with the rest of his clothing. Oscar noticed the insistence of his friend in fixing the scarf.

"It is a signal in this situations."

He knew the cinema Odeon for its reputation, he had never entered. It was a porn cinema, attended by boys and old men, and now he knew that it also was a crossroad for mercenary exchanges.

It was nine when they arrived at the cinema. They parked in a desert square, next to the Dome, and headed towards the entrance. Oscar went in first, and got near the cash register.

"One!"

A fat, peaceful and bored man peered through the glass and handed the paper with a sly smile. He followed the operation from a distance, as agreed, and after a few seconds he followed Oscar.

"One ticket, please. Has it started yet?"

"What difference does it make, for what you need."

"Can you tell me where can I find the bathroom?"

"Don't you know, bottom left, behind the curtain. Are you here to shoot drugs?"

"I don't even think about it."

"Ah, well! I understand. Go, go . . . you will not miss the best."

In the hall, just below the screen, some silhouettes could be seen. He recognized Oscar's in the first rows, and got there. He stopped just behind him and sat down. He heard from time to time a little unnatural cough, he wondered whether they were signals, because the cough coming from a side was followed by another from the other side. The moans from the screen were a counterpoint to coughs and soft steps. He hardly noticed that Oscar had changed his place, sitting next to a tiny figure of thick curly hair. The two stood up and walked towards the exit. There you go, he thought, and followed them. The ticket clerk saw the two going out, and when he saw him, he said: "Don't you like the movie?"

"Good bye."

"Yes, well . . . To you, sir."

He saw the two slip away towards the square: they got into the car and went away.

He decided to spend the time hanging out near the Cathedral, which never failed to fascinate him with its essential geometry. He walked towards the sea, sat on a wall and let himself be enchanted by the sound of the waves. He did not realize how long he had been absorbed, he thought it was time to head back to the square, just in case Oscar had come back.

Oscar was in the car waiting for him.

"Already back!"

"Get in, he was not . . . He was not clean, you know?"

"Sorry, no . . ."

"A toxic, better not to take risks. We go to the station."

It was ten o'clock. The station looked sad and desolate like the places out of season. A couple of people were sitting on the wooden benches. Oscar looked around, he watched him from the glass beyond the tracks. The loudspeaker announced a train, the two men got on the second track: they looked tired with their humble clothes, perhaps they were workers returning home. The train came rattling and hissing, the two got on board and the train departed. The station seemed even more melancholic.

The station master entered his office.

Oscar went to the toilets, he disappeared for a few seconds. Then he saw him coming out with a young man in jeans and shirt, long hair tied behind his neck, a cigarette between his lips and a newspaper in his hand. The young man gesticulated, he seemed reluctant. They stopped in front of the exit, he saw Oscar pointing in the direction of the square. They disappeared.

He tried to imagine what would happen between them, but he withdrew immediately from that thought.

He went to the toilets, which he imagined desert, and there he found a fine gentleman, forty years old, who followed him with the eyes. He was about to go back over his steps, but, instead, he walked mechanically into one of the two toilettes and shut the door behind him, in apprehension. The distinguished gentleman had sensed his hesitation.

When he came out, the distinguished gentleman was on the threshold, as if wanting to block the passage.

"Have you got a lighter?"

"I don't smoke!"

He lied. The gentleman, encouraged by an answer he evidently didn't expect, insisted.

"Can you tell me the time?"

"It's twenty past ten."

"Are you waiting for anyone? If you are alone, we could have a chat, so, to pass the time."

He felt uneasy, he lingered.

"Why not . . . What are you doing at the station at this time?"

"Come on, do not tell me that you don't quite understand . . . Is it the first time that you . . ."

"I've come here are other times . . . to catch trains."

"I see. I never noticed you before. Let me introduce myself: Annibale."

"Umberto."

"Tonight, then, what are you doing?"

"You wouldn't believe it, I'm here out of curiosity, I accompanied a friend."

"The one with the mustache?"

"Himself. He'll be back soon, I hope."

"Oh, certainly. These things do not take long."

They walked up and down on the platform, the look of a porter followed them sardonically: when the two passed under his nose, he attacked in his teeth a honey-like old times tune: "Amàaado mìiooo, staseraomàaiii . . ."

The distinguished gentleman felt his discomfort.

"Do you prefer we leave the station?"

"Maybe it's better."

In front of the station stood a woman waiting, a dog, melancholically disoriented and alone, and the dominating night.

"Do you live here in town?"

"I come from another place. I have long lived in the North, for twenty years, then I let it all go, family, work, friends who would not understand, and I came down here: new job, new house, no friends, except those of a one night stand. Since then a lot of things have changed in my life, first of all I began to live by night. Believe it or not, but the night lives much more than the apparent chaos of the day, despite its apparent immobility, the night is . . . fluid, mobile. One can perceive voices that are living a different life. If the day needs restraint, with the night you cannot bluff . . . The day is reason, the night is instinct, intuition, fear. What you see has little importance by night: at night you hear, you smell, you sniff as animals do . . . Do you see that dog? Well, we're friends. We became friends when, one night, he asked my help, yes, exactly. I was walking as every night, wandering alone in the usual places, suddenly I felt a call, not a bark or a howl, no . . . I felt that someone was calling me, was launching a desperate cry for help! I felt it as a stab of pain here, in the center of the chest, and then a force pushed me towards an unknown direction. The night was very quiet, it was winter. I followed my instinct and

I arrived here, where we are now, and I met Fidel . . . the name I gave to the dog. So he followed me, with no need to speak or anything else; we wandered, I went first and he followed me. And every night you will find him here, punctual and faithful like not even the best lovers . . . So . . . this is the night."

"Have you ever been afraid?"

"Often, I would say every night, but you see, you cannot escape it, it would be, you know . . . useless."

"I do not understand."

"It was just the denial of fear that forced me to live an artificial life. I was afraid, sure, a lot, but I thought it was a feeling, an ignoble emotion, contemptible for a man, and so I escaped in every way from it.

But it always found me and claimed its right to be there. Little by little I learned to make room for it, I could no longer resist it. You cannot win over fear, you need to cheat it, to seduce it, you have to tame it every day, and model yourself on it . . . I am often afraid at night, I happened to live dangerous situations, but I learned to take it into account. Fear simply is there, it has to be there . . . but this makes me less afraid, you know?"

"I think I understand. It's getting late and my friend has not returned yet, I begin to feel a strange premonition."

"Listen carefully to your premonition, it probably wants to communicate something important for you or your friend . . . Now I must leave, you know . . . my usual rounds. It's been a pleasure speaking with you, I hope to see you again."

"I hope so. Good luck!"

The distinguished gentleman walked away with no hurry in the direction of the harbor. He saw him disappear into the night, that was much darker in the alleys around the harbor. Fidel remained at his place under a lamplight a little longer. Then he sniffed the night, he pointed the darkness in which his friend was getting lost, then yawned, stood up, yawned again, and finally he trotted on the trail of his friend.

Fragment 7

"SO, YOU WERE SAYING YOU knew the victim. How come you knew him?"

"As I was saying, we were friends, we had known each other for years."

"What kind of friendship?"

"Just friendship, Marshal."

"Why were you at the station at that hour, and how did you know that the victim would go back there?"

"We got there together, by his car."

"Together, uh? And you want me to believe that there was just a friendship between you? You must admit that this is strange, inconclusive, is it?"

"I repeat: I was curious, I accompanied him because . . . I wanted to know more about . . ."

"About what?"

"About his life, or rather about that part of his life from which I was excluded and which Oscar never talked about, that's all."

"Um . . . weird. Your friend surely had things to hide, because, you see, in the pocket of his jacket we found this note, it seems a warning, I read it: "*This is what appens to the bastards like you do not tach children*", he meant "do not touch them", obviously."

"What do you mean?"

"It is very likely that your friend took pleasure in, you know, do certain things with kids, with minors, you see what I mean? That must have given much annoyance to someone. When you saw your friend go away, you could see his companion's face, would you be able to say what age he was, roughly?"

"It was dark, and then I was pretty far at that moment."

"Well, we intend to develop this line and we'll see what comes out of it."

"Could I know where my friend has been brought?"

"Currently he is at the morgue at the magistrate's disposal. Ah, it is very likely that you'll be called for the recognition, I tell you so that you have the goodness not to leave the city for the next twenty-four hours, then we will have to investigate and clarify once for good you position. For now you can go, please."

He returned to the station without a reason. He paced uneasily under the arcades hoping that Oscar came back: he had to return sooner or later, he thought to himself. A car stopped a few paces away, a little and stout man got out of it and walked hurriedly towards the woman who, meanwhile, was still waiting. They chattered, she moved, followed by the little man, who was wildly gesticulating.

The woman stopped, examined him over and asked for a light. Finally they moved towards the car, the little man before, the woman behind him, calmly swaying. They disappeared.

The arrival of a train was announced, one of those coming from far away and going even further. He lit a cigarette and inhaled deeply, he looked up and noticed that an unfinished moon was performing on the night and the city. It was midnight, he decided it was time to go home, it was useless to wait for someone whom you cannot find any more, he thought.

Epilogue

HE BRUSHED HIS TEETH, DRANK a glass of water and spit out in the basin.

He lingered in front of the mirror: he breathed against it till the reflected image vanished, wrapped in a homogeneous fog. This, during a while, eased the anguish in which he felt entrapped. He came out of the bathroom: "No television tonight", he thought.

He slipped in the unmade bed, tried to read some pages and then turned off the light. Salomé, his Persian cat, curled up into the hollow of his knees and began happily to purr.

He fell into a sleep full of dreams: an unknown village, a mysterious temple, strange signs of an enigmatic alphabet, and the moon suggesting ancient and immutable truths.

And he was not going to see Oscar any more.

The little brother

· ·

MANY YEARS AGO, I DO not remember exactly how many, the last of my four brothers was born. His name was Teresio.

The novelty, that had left me indifferent at the time, reached me while I was on holiday in a Tuscany village, a cluster of houses, some of which were crumbling, gathering along a single road paved with loose stones. The village was located on the side of a mountain that had been leveled to make way for the houses.

The college in which I stayed for the most part of the year, had moved for the holidays into the thick walls of the village's seminary, and on the month of August of that year it gave hospitality to fifty boys aged between twelve and eighteen.

After all these years I have only scraps of memories of those days spent reading, attending religious services, making trips and keeping long silences trying to grasp the meaning of things.

Without being really aware, I was creating and harmonizing in my boyish imagination a representation of reality that, after a few years, would have cracked, forcing me to rethink and rebuild the foundations of a new, and different in many respects, order of things.

I cannot say why, but this morning, while browsing the newspaper, some moments of that remote and faded holiday are returning to my mind: places, situations, games, faces of some classmates mingled with the memory of that event, the birth of a brother who is gone.

In an attempt to reconstruct as closely as possible the map of quiet streets that kept together in a disjointed and seemingly hopeless labyrinth, memory cannot but be supported by imagination. I must admit, indeed, that of the whole web of streets I can only remember the largest and longest one, the street that held together all the other, serving as a reference for the villagers and as demarcation line between two rows of houses facing each other along what was pompously called "the avenue", when in fact it only was a long narrow gut in which even for the sun it was difficult to penetrate.

To come out of the village it was necessary to go down a dirt road disentangling as a snake, whose coils were camouflaged among the green woods, without mentioning the countless paths, the mule tracks departing from it, reconnecting at the bottom, which seemed a much more fascinating and mysterious trip than a walk along the edges of the big road.

One of them was my favorite. It led to a thick wood of oak trees in which small animals, snakes and birds nested. They used to flee as soon as the excited shouts of the children flooded the forest. The children scattered in the thickness, they concealed themselves and disappeared from the view of the "superiors", the priests who accompanied us on those walks, so that from the side of the path only voices and screams could be heard, as if we were into a speaking wood, infested by joyful presences.

It was easy to intermingle among bushes and rocks, losing the sense of everyday's things and the distances that measured the relationships between people, the wood was the place of possible transgression, a dimension where one could give time and its pacing away, and look beyond the edge as in a negative picture showing the reverse.

On the morning when they announced to me that my family was enriched by a new component, the air was fresh and crisp, a persistent breeze had cleared the sky with a thin layer that veiled it, and the colors were bright and saturated.

One of the priests called me. I temporary left my games and learned of the birth of my new brother. I sketched a smile and a look of surprise, but without great enthusiasm.

They also announced to me the name of the newcomer: Teresio. A strange and unusual name in my family, excepting the sad precedent of an aunt who died very young leaving two small children, and whose name was just Teresa.

The newcomer's name began to bounce obsessively into my mind, and the speculation about how the birth had happened and about the new family structure, along with assumptions on the features of my brother, monopolized my imagination. Despite my age, I was fifteen, and the birth of other brothers before and after me, my knowledge about childbirth, all that preceded and followed it, was vague and elusive. When my third brother was born, for instance, I passed the time waiting on the steps of a church, in the middle of a scorching August afternoon, playing and chanting large parts of what was, although I did not know it by that time, the Gregorian liturgy of the dead. My constant attendance at catechism classes, my constant presence in the parish as an altar boy, which had often led me to serve masses for the dead, my relationship with the pastor of the parish, all these circumstances made me a supposed expert on liturgical texts, and of the right melodies for every different circumstances. But Vatican II was still to come and the prayers in Latin compelled us to unremitting acts of faith and submission to a meaning entirely unknown.

Well, today I can say that, while my third brother was coming in the world, I had no better than to wish him an early Mass for the dead.

In Teresio's case, however, things went differently. I began to feel excited and impatient, eager to stand as soon as possible face to face with the "little brother"—this was the name used in family to appoint Teresio, and was kept in place of the baptismal name for the entire period of his brief permanence in this world. He died very young, in fact, after only three months.

What memory has erased beyond repair is the exact time when I was in front of my little brother for the first time. I cannot remember although I strain my imagination.

Of the period of my life with my brother I can only remember a few situations that were carved in my mind as evidence of real existence in the family of that person, because after so many years the forgetfulness has eroded the margins of an existence that had only the time to announce itself before fading away. I keep the memory of the day of his death—the night, actually—and that of his funeral.

When the little brother was born, at home there was not much space. We were six, but my mother loved children, had wanted many, and the last too was received with pleasure—that is what mother used to say. What she, perhaps out of modesty, did not mention, was that actually the childbirths after the first were unsuccessful attempts: she wanted at all costs a girl who would not come and, unfortunately for her, who would never come, since she gave birth only to boys.

Twenty years ago at home we were all children, beginning with those who are now on their way, and the moment of the dedicated to "the bath" for the little brother was the hub of family life, the place of tenderness offered with words, looks and gestures that had my brother as their sole object. We moved excited around his little reddish body, his face wrinkled into a touching smile; we brothers competed for him with the eyes, we just touched him with the tips of our fingers in a frantic desire to attract his attention, satisfied if we succeeded in making his head turn or in tearing a moan as a sign of response to our solicitations.

After being properly rubbed and shaken, mother showed the bundle in all its redness as a trophy and we kept competing to attract his attention. At this point mother intervened in a Solomon's manner, leaving us all unhappy saying that the child needed to sleep and bidding us to stay silent. With our great delusion, we were deprived of our toy. Things fell hopelessly after a while, when the little brother began to show the first signs of a misunderstood and obscure illness, that in little more than a month would erase forever from the memory of the world the appearance of a human being who showed signs of a discomfort, or inability to adapt to a reality experienced as threatening.

The fact is that the little brother refused to eat food, he just decided he was not to be fed—though a will like that may seem implausible in a child two months old—he had decided to die, this was, in short, the apparent truth.

We ran breathlessly from a hospital to another, but all proved useless, the attempts to take the little brother away from death showed their complete uselessness in the facts. And the brother, in his hurry to escape from the hassle of staying alive and perhaps fighting against a residual desire to survive, lost weight every day, until he showed signs of irreversible decay. He looked like a ghost, in his absurd thinness.

It was a November night when brother let go.

I had been heralded about the severity of the baby's condition by an uncle, the widower of Teresa, who I had met in the street as I walked home from college. It was a Saturday.

In the house hung the gloomy atmosphere of the tragedy that was happening and that would have death as its inevitable epilogue, as doctors said. Their advise was in fact to bring home the pitiful bundle, as long as a breath of survival was left.

And brother was there, a pitiful thing now. He seemed to disappear in the king-sized bed on which mother had laid him. We stood watching his agony.

Mother was sitting next to little brother, and from time to time she moistened his lips parched by medicines and thirst, which had reduced him to skin and bones.

Nothing similar had ever befallen on our family. The spectacle of suffering and despair that followed the death of that little being, who had lived so little time but enough intensely to experiment a distillate of pain, the quintessence of the condition that binds us together, deeply disturbed me, and not only because it was about my brother. The plot of affections in which we recognize a deep and lasting connection began, in his case, to loosen and shatter as soon as brother had to leave the house to wander from one hospital to another.

I was stunned, in fact, by the combination of pain and sense of tragedy that bounced from one relative to another. And then the pity and the sense of ineluctability that characterized until the end the relationship, physical too, that united mother and child. Mother held little brother in her arms yet for a long time and permitted to no one else to lay him down in the skimpy white coffin that henceforth would replace her arms. I felt that there was already a sense of death in the bond that had united in this world mother and son: the very short parabola beginning with his birth—actually, with death from the uterine dimension—had exhausted in the short space of three months, with the death of the body. The mother had expelled him, and along with the possibility of life she anticipated for him the possibility of death, as if the mother bore in herself, intimately fused, the power of life and death.

She had represented a shelter in which, away from possible trouble, a being would develop. Then he was expelled, who knows how violently, and what awaited him was certainly much of an enigma.

Against the light, through the half-closed door of my room, I saw and heard mother, with the bundle in her arms, talking to little brother as if he were able to understand and, most poignant, as if he were alive. Actually he had just died, and mother's moaning laments woke me up, placing under my eyes the scene of that "Pietà".

The night passed. Death, in his incessant travel, had stopped at our house and had decided to settle, at least for now.

I remember that the next day our house became a place of pilgrimage, painful for somebody, pitiful for others, for some others only a duty. The rooms filled with people and faint murmurs. I had never watched death in the face, until then, and I was wandering about the house among people I barely knew and relatives who from time to time glanced melancholically at me.

Then I remember that the priest came along. He blessed, he assured those present about the real and ultimate destination of little brother, who, he said, "in this moment is in Heaven, in the glory of God the Father, angel among the angels, and from there he watches you and prays for you. This thought comfort you in this time of sorrow."

I remember thinking: yeah, it was a thought, just a thought, something like a remote possibility that nothing and no one can confirm or deny, and certainly did not justify or explain the destiny that had drawn the short life of little brother. Who decided that? and why? What was meaning of that life? Does it make any sense to be catapulted into a hostile dimension without even the opportunity to protest, to complain, to ask for that? And then, ask to whom? If it is true, as it is written in the Hebrew Scriptures, that he who saves one life saves the entire world, one could think that with the death of little brother the whole world would die with him. But the world has continued to go on without him. Maybe it was just the will of the world who never wanted him, and got rid of him as a hindrance.

And what would he do as an angel, as the priest said: would he remain for eternity in the presence of a Being against whom he dared not look up, or give out a groan to blame Him for an ungenerous life that appeared and disappeared with the speed of lightning?

Little brother could have been everything or nothing, he could have the world in his hands. He could have cut with his presence the hard peel of history revealing to mankind the language of angels and the harmony of infinite. He could have raised over the misery of the human condition and lead men to an Eden full of wishes. But he could as well touch the depths of misery, confine himself in a compound of folly, wandering among his peers as in an eternal exile from himself and the from world. He could have known the sorrow of repayment, and the grip of regret, he might have touched deceptions of love and the lure of lust.

He could, but he had not the time . . .

When the priest took his leave, the people began to swarm up through the stairs. Mother went to the little inert body and kept that wrapping in an embrace that, even briefly, melted them into one body. Then she put little brother in the coffin and let the undertaker do his job. He took possession of the coffin without much grace.

After the funeral, the body was taken to the cemetery and buried underground, in the midst of an endless line of iron crosses, in what looked like a macabre cornfield.

For some time the cross was all that remained of little brother, then also the latest sign of his passage was swept away by bulldozers and cement castings, which erected on that piece of land anonymous five-storey chapels . . . better the ground.

Dirty room

· · · · · · · · · · · · · · · ·

HE WAS RETURNING HOME FOLLOWING the slow rhythm of the steps, while his confused thoughts overlapped. His favorite occupation, when he walked, was observing people, scanning their looks to capture a reflection of the concerns that gave life to them.

That morning he had come out to attend to some matters, he had gone to the doctor's and then to the chemist's. Now an unspecified number of flower beds, trees, shops, a tobacconist's, a hotel and a level crossing which in that moment barred the way to cars and motorcycles, to pedestrians, to their thoughts and to their daily pain, separated him from home. On one side there was his house made of thoughts, on the other side there was his real house, one large room, often dirty.

Near the tobacconist's he saw, across the street, an acquaintance. He crossed the road with the intention of stopping to chat. He stood before him with his hands in the pockets of a worn-out jacket, to protect them from the February icy wind.

"Hi, how was your stay in the capital?"

The acquaintance was seated on a wooden untidy bench. While he was speaking, he could feel in the guy who sat in front of him a deaf, hostile reticence. Giovanni, called Zazzera, had stayed in the Capital for three months, hosted by "someone", as he called him, who, in exchange for some joints, a bed and the illusion of good life, asked from him some "pieces", paintings—Zazzera was a decent painter, when he managed to keep his feet on the ground without "tripping". When "someone" had been arrested for his dishonest deals, Zazzera had to return, so to speak.

"I do not want to talk about that", Zazzera said, and he remained seated. He wore a wool hat well pulled down, with which he concealed his total baldness.

He sat next to Zazzera and for a while they remained glued shoulder to shoulder. When silence between the two became embarrassing, he began to feel a profound sense of estrangement. Why do I stay here? What keeps me with this person, on this bench? He wondered.

An insidious anguish began to pursue him. So he stood up in front of Zazzera. With his eyes ranging in all directions, he began to follow the chaotic flood of kids who were leaving school, spreading on the streets and converging on the gardens where the benches were. The students were advancing in one compact direction, as if moved by a common will.

Within that shapeless and multicolored organism, the bright colors of sweaters, of wind-jackets, of blouses stood out. girls wore wool hats, gloves and pastel color overalls that marvelously blended with their faces reddened by the cold. He let himself be fascinated by that sight, and began to follow with the eyes a little girl in particular. The look became a thread of thoughts that condensed around the girl's face, her gypsy dark complexion, and her stern, sharp look, loaded, he thought, with enticing intentions. He followed her for a long while, stuck to her eyes and to the lines of her body, then he saw her disappearing behind a screen of road signs, parked cars and people that crowded the sidewalk.

Without an explanation, he grabbed Zazzera's arm and forcing him to follow. Zazzera did not understand, but he left him lead. They walked together and when they found the girl, he told Zazzera: "Do you see that girl?" Zazzera looked forwards, then looked at him and smiled, and the smile became an irritating laugh when Zazzera guessed the reason for that unscheduled walk.

"What are your intentions?"

"I do not know . . . I was thinking about following her, maybe to stop her . . . I don't know."

"And what am I doing, do you need help?"

"No . . . I thought . . . yes, in fact, two . . ."

"I think you'll have to attend to it alone, I'm not going to be your support, and then she's only a little chick, she must be fifteen, sixteen? Forget it . . . you won't get a damn from her."

"Yes, maybe you're right, but if you help me . . . maybe . . ."

"Maybe what? And why me?"

"So . . . I do not know, I thought . . ."

"Do me the favour: I don't give a damn shit about you . . . you and that . . . ah, fuck off. Take care." Until then he had managed to keep between himself and the girl a safe distance, now he thought it was time to do the most daring move, but he was by no means sure that the maneuver would succeed. Still he had to stop her.

Once he had lost and found her in the crowd, he continued to chase the girl with his eyes, he began a slow and uncertain march of approach which, in his intention, was to lead him to the girl. The girl, who now walked about ten steps forward, stopped, unexpectedly turned back and seemed to head in his direction—in a dark corner of his conscience he said, who knows why, against him. However, he interpreted the girl's about-turn as a positive sign, and could not help but believe that the girl had obeyed an obscure impulse prompted by a message that reached her through the invisible web that his desire had been weaving around her. He believed, in short, he had been able to ride the girl's will.

She stopped, leaned against a pole, took the phone from a backpack and began to fumble with the buttons.

"She's really pretty", he thought. He kept staring at her. She wore a fuchsia wool hat and candy pink sneakers, that he found irresistible. Her profile was smooth, with a nose that drifted slightly upwards, and two naturally crimson lips—that could not be glossy lips, he thought. And how tall she was. Her thin legs, wrapped in a pair of dark jeans torn at the knees, seemed to never end, and the ease with which she leaned her body to the pole gave the impression that she had no weight, even that she was leaning to the pole to avoid rising in flight.

How he would have liked to have Zazzera at his side now, his presence would somehow have comforted him, because he felt the nagging feeling that he was about to abandon the enterprise. He was afraid, a knot in the center of the chest which annihilated his will.

The girl leaning to the pole was excitedly fingering the buttons of her phone: after the SMS, it was the turn of the incoming and outgoing calls. He studied the girl's facial expressions, the movements of her hands, the posture of her head, now soft, now tense, her body alert or abandoned against the pole, and he believed he could guess from those signs the girl's mood. He could tell if she was speaking with a friend, with an acquaintance, a close friend or someone that called for the first time. He believed he could guess that.

From the location where he was barricaded, behind the tanks that marked the entrance to a bar, he had not stopped, not even for a second, studying the moves of the girl, but he felt growing inside impatience and anxiety, that was impulse and hesitation, appeal to a shaky desire for action and allegiance to the demon of fear. Finally he decided to reveal himself, he left the leafy trench and decided he would walk up and down along a stretch of the pavement. Luckily he could stop and pretend to look at shop windows or to read posters, so the first two steps under the indifferent gaze of the girl, though still shaken, were useful to be brave and be able to say that, basically, the sidewalk was of everyone, everyone could walk it without having to justify, or arousing suspects, and if someone, like him, had nothing better to do, he was free to hang around, even free to count the tiles of the pavement, if he wished to, or even stand still at an angle to categorize by color, type or plate, the cars passing by.

There followed a third and fourth passage. He had the time to memorize the sequence of windows on that side of the sidewalk and to calculate, with good approximation, the frequency with which two birds perched on the ledge in front of the building would move from side to side of the road. For the girl, still busy with the cell, he was still a shadow, a subliminal fleeting image.

At the sixth passage he stumbled right under the amused gaze of the girl and never incident was more favorable because, although he was almost dislocating his ankle, and when he resumed his balance on his legs he would have liked a chasm to open there under his feet and swallow him, it is nevertheless true that the mishap made him visible to the girl, who looked at him with pity and fun, and followed for a bit his twisted walk.

He returned to shelter behind the tanks, but it was not a withdraw, it was rather a recoil, a tactical retreat that gave him the opportunity to set in order, to absorb the temporary beating in view of a renewed assault.

He stood in front of a shoe store window, just opposite to the girl, who looked up, recognized him, chuckled and returned to her cell. But he did not move from there, he held the position and began to look at the girl with an entirely new audacity, and more and more often her looks crossed his.

When finally she put the phone into a pocket of the backpack, he was so focused on a detail of her cap that he did not notice that the girl was standing in front of him, studying him as he were an alien.

"Are you going to remain stock-still here all day?"

He shook himself but did not understand the words of the girl, but he felt that she had spoken to him.

"Why do not we have a walk? Come, accompany me."

He followed the girl like a robot, staying two steps behind her.

Only when he realized what was happening, he managed to give his mind a well-deserved break, and when the girl, amused, asked him to pace side by side with her, he even found the determination to speak to her.

"What's your name?"

"Nicoletta, but I prefer to be called Samantha, it is cool."

"Which grade do you attend?"

"The second, high school."

By a quick calculation, he realized that Zazzera was wrong about the age of the girl, after all, now he had the opportunity to observe her close, despite a heavy coat of makeup, or perhaps because of that, the girl appeared to be older than her age, she seemed twenty, or so. Proximity, however, had not dissolved the aura of grace and charm that had immediately impressed him, though doubts arose about the genuineness of her face.

"May I ask you a question?"

"Shoot."

"Sure you're not going to offend?"

"If it is not bullshit, go ahead."

"No . . . it's just out of curiosity, but if it bothers you . . . in short . . . if you do not like . . ."

"Shit, how long will you make it? I told you to shoot."

She was vigorously chewing a gum, and occasionally she sniffed and, he discovered, she had an odd tic that obliged her to turn up her nose lifting alternately now the right, now the left nostril.

But her profile appeared, despite everything, of an unspeakable delicacy, and reminded him of a Rodin's sculpture he had seen at the *Musée d'Orsay*, when he was Paris.

"You're just so . . . your skin, I mean, you're dark-skinned?"

She laughed noisily and looked at him as if he were a naive.

"UVA lamp, three times a week . . . it costs me an eye."

The phone rang, she seemed to forget that she had a companion and devoted herself with zeal to the call.

For him, a truce.

He felt mixed and confused, and since the girl was ignoring him, absorbed by a dialogue made of monosyllables, of short grunts and half-sentences, he devoted himself to his thoughts.

Beautiful, she was beautiful, he thought, she was attractive, but it was not enough. Not that this was not enough in a girl, damn, no, it was not that. Words were not enough. Words to express the idea of beauty, frozen in the bottom of his dirty room, that this girl seemed to have evoked against her will.

For someone like him who called himself—by the way, with a touch of rhetoric—a pilgrim of beauty, a woman, especially if beautiful, was not simply a body, but a tangible impression of the divine endowed with a great power.

Pretty, she was pretty, he thought, and even aware, and that mix of pink and fuchsia, the balance between the dark red of the lips, the amber of the earrings, and her gypsy complexion, excited him. And the fact that she had chosen him, that she had spoken to him when she could have ignored him, despite his clumsy attempts to make himself noticed, made him proud, but just a little bit. He dared not think of it, and certainly would not have had the courage to tell it to the girl, but he was already in love, bewitched, head over heels in love with her.

"Agreed, ok . . . yes, but be quiet, you know that there is a special rate for you . . . yes, as usual . . . the usual time, Oh well . . . bye bye."

She put down the phone and turned to look at him as though seeing him now for the first time.

"Sorry, I do not remember, have we already made an agreement?"

"I could not . . . know . . . what?"

"No no, forget it . . . Come on, we're turning this way."

The girl collected her chewing-gum in a handkerchief and replaced it immediately with a new one.

"Do you want one?"

"No, thanks."

He realized that the girl was driving toward the city center, an ancient and falling urban center almost completely abandoned, a maze of twisting alleyways, often malodorous because of the sewer manholes, from which it was not unusual to peep one of those big mice they call "zoccole." He followed the girl as an altar boy, obedient and unconscious, his neck rigid and his eyes moving. She was intent to crumple her chewing gum, to reboot her hair with her fingers and tormenting a doll, a teddy bear hanging from the strap of her backpack. He thought that perhaps he should say something. She thought that maybe it was time to ask him something.

"Do you live here, nearby?"

"Yes . . . but just for a few months still, we are moving to another neighborhood, my mother bought a house."

"Ah, how nice . . ."

"Not really . . . I feel good here, it is a quiet zone, and I'm always alone at home."

"And your parents?"

"I see my mother very little, you know . . . work, and thank Goodness, so I don't find her constantly getting on my tits . . ."

"It's a nice long walk every day, from home to school, eh?"

"It's not a problem, there is always someone who comes to fetch me and takes me."

"You have many friends?"

"Friends? People I know, people I see sometimes."

The phone rang again—a wacky ring tone, a vulgar laugh. As she slipped off the phone from the pocket of her backpack, he felt a surge of annoyance at the idea that she would once again ignore, exclude, forget him for who knows how long, to keep up with the disturber in turn's chatter. He wanted to ask the girl to cut the call, but he dared not, he had not that right, at least for now. Maybe later, when things between them would have taken a different turn, perhaps he could claim more prompt attention from the girl, but not now.

"Listen, how do I have to tell you: I'm not going to see you anymore, fuck off, you understand? . . . Oh yeah, now you say these things. Why not . . . how?! You've just got a face like a bum, you know? yes . . . yes, give me a break, who do you want to fuc . . . No . . . I've already tol . . . Yes? . . . It was . . . for the last time . . . but what does it mean . . . No . . . I said . . . some things with you . . . No! I said no, I don't do that!"

She closed the phone with an angry gesture, spat the chewing gum and stared at her companion, his ingenuous and clumsy attitude: he wanted her to believe he was innocent, that, unlike the others, he was there only because he liked the idea of a stroll and a chat with her, poor idiot?

He had an intimate motion of rebellion and indignation at the idea that some unknown villain, certainly a great wretched . . . a rude peasant, could disturb the serenity of his . . . of his girlfriend, he was to say, but he stopped in time. Yes, but it was only a matter of time, he thought, what now he only dared to hope would soon turn into reality, and then no disturbers around.

But now she was angry, his almost girlfriend, his promise of happiness within reach, his living sculpture, what could he do to make her smile again, to make her turn again towards him that look of amber and malice?

"Do you have a chewing gum for me?"

"Just two are left."

She threw the empty pack, then she kicked it off with a shot of the tip. As in a step of flamenco, the leg lifted backwards and then stopped right at the impact with the pack, whose trajectory led it to bounce a few inches from the muzzle of a cat, who was dozing crouched at the foot of a short flight of steps, one of those not uncommon to find before the front doors of the houses in that part of the town. The cat jumped up confused, let out a slight mewing and dashed to hide elsewhere.

"I'm almost there, I live there."

There is no time, no time, he thought, now or never, I must ask her. Yes, but how, what do I say, he thought, words do not come, never come when you need them. He tried to mentally set a beginning, then another and another yet, but it seemed that words did not tie up to each other, did not connect in a logical and significant sequence, in the only chain that could say what he hoped, what he wished.

"At six I have an appointment at the beautician's . . . what if I become blonde? Maybe not completely, I rather thought about streaks, first a lightening, I cannot certainly have streaks with this hair . . . although with the lights . . . what do you think?"

He did not think anything, now he could not.

"Listen, we can meet at five o'clock, my mother is at work and nobody will disturb us. We'll do things quietly, I think half an hour should be enough, then I'll make some phone calls and at six I'll be in time for the beautician. So, is it okay for you?"

Any time would be okay, if it meant seeing her again, near her, talking to her, of course. And how easy it had been, he thought comforted, easier than he dared to hope: the girl's confidence had spared him painful stammering, her initiative was holding out happiness on a silver plate garnished with malice and seduction.

"So, let me tell you my prices: thirty for a blowjob, fifty for the normal, and eighty for the ass, which do you prefer?"

How cute she was now, staring at him and smiling again, and . . . What?

Suddenly he felt that he could not open his mouth without stammering, without being tormented again by that painful incident that had troubled his childhood, nailing him to his clumsiness.

"W . . . what d . . . do you m . . . mean?"

"These are my rates: thirty if you want a blowjob, fifty if you want to fuck normally and eighty if you want to do it from behind."

"B . . . but . . . what are you t . . . ta . . . talking about?"

"Ah, but then I was right to think that you're a little bit of an asshole, I suspected that from the beginning. Listen, I have no time to lose, I've already lost enough. Let's do this way: I live here, this is my house, now you know, when you've decided you can come and see me, and I assure you that there is no risk. Take care and . . . fuck you."

She disappeared slamming the door of the main entrance, he stood motionless to absorb the bump. He believed he understood the girl's words correctly, but he was unable to pronounce the word, the only sufficiently concise and appropriate: bitch.

She was a bitch. She was . . . was . . . yes, in short, that thing there? Had he understood well? Yes, he knew well: thirty . . . fifty . . . eighty . . . : images of dissoluteness and bestial coitus and . . . and I?, he thought.

He just had to leave, and on the contrary he stared at the door, that big rock called Sesame that no magic formula would open, if not a few ten euro's bills. He had to leave, but he did not. Instead, he beat angrily against the door.

He beat his disappointment, frustration, deception of which he felt to be a victim: deception of beauty, of flattery, of seduction, of expectations. And then the self-delusion, the belief that beauty and goodness could embody in one form, that sensitive harmony was just the reflection, albeit faint, of something else, superior.

He had to leave, and instead he rang for long imagining that the girl returned, that she promised she would delete all the phone numbers and keep only his, that, for him, she would change her life. But he just had to leave.

His staying behind the entrance door began to attract cats and nosey parkers, some cars slowed down and then drove away, a kid in the neighborhood, accustomed to living on the street, sat on a step to enjoy the show. Then, as a sinister omen, a huge, long, interminable and black car arrived and stopped across the alley. It seemed a spaceship. No silhouette could be seen through the tinted windows. He did not notice it, he remained still stack to his illusions and to the bell. He did not even notice that, through the curtains of a window, the girl waved her hand as a sign of agreement in direction of the spaceship. Then that harmonious mass of iron, rubber and glass moved, first a few meters backwards, then forwards. It stopped behind him and turned off the engine. The driver's window lowered as slowly as a sloth, framing a large bald head, a Mongol mustache, a purple nose decorated with a wart and two watery eyes of a light and vague color.

"Go home, listen to me."

It seemed the uncertain voice of a teenager who still cannot master the low and acute tones.

"Can you hear me? I said go home, forget it."

He turned and leaned against the door, he stared at the stranger, he seemed to smile, then he began kicking the door with his heel, and every kick left a thick, half-moon shaped trace. He kicked and stared at the big head framed by the window.

"Why you don't understand?"

He thought the girl would yield to his insistence, he thought that no one before had shown such tenacity, that no one had done crazy things for her, that no one, like him, had abdicated his own sake, and no one was capable of loving her as he could. He did not even doubt that all this could annoy the girl.

"You've got to go, you understand, damn it!"

The driver, who meanwhile had got out of the ship, seemed a little green men, short and stocky, one would have found it hard to believe that he could steer a vehicle apparently so complicated.

"Have you understood what I said?"

But he gave him no more time. He hit him with two fists in the stomach and one on the nose, then he grabbed the boy by the shoulders, shook him, pulled him and then threw him against the door. When the boy who sat enjoying the show noticed a copious stream of blood flowing from the right nostril of the boy, he stood up and walked away alarmed.

"I told you to let go, to return home."

The little man thought it appropriate to confirm his intentions: another fist in the stomach, a slap on the neck, since the boy had finally doubled up in pain, and a kick in the side, because the boy had finally collapsed at the man's feet.

"I'll go now, see that you leave, too."

The little man slipped into the starship, the window raised as slowly as a sloth, the boy tried to recover.

There was a fountain in the alley a few steps further, the boy dipped a couple of paper towels and tried to absorb the trickle of blood, and washed his face. The water was cold and made him shiver. He looked around, the streets seemed deserted.

When he was on the main street, an unspecified number of flower beds, trees, buildings, shops, a tobacconist's, a hotel, and a level crossing, which at that time was closed, separated him from home. On one side there was his house made of thoughts, on the other side there was his real house, but he could not tell which one was dirtier.

Holiday

. . . .

THEY HAD BEEN IN THE park for three days and Sandro had not been able to stay alone for more than ten minutes, despite the fact that he wished to obtain from that holiday in the mountains the opportunity to enjoy time for himself alone. Ivan, Sandro and Umberto had gone on holiday together only because they shared the same destination, the National Park. Ivan and Umberto had known each other since the college. Sandro knew Umberto, who introduced him to Ivan. In the car none of the three uttered a word: up to the point they were, only a healthy quarrel would have taken back a relative tranquility.

As usual, Ivan had decided for all: excursion down to the lake for the next day. Sandro, on the contrary, wanted to climb up the slope and did not mean to follow the other two.

They were walking along the lake. At that time in the evening the surface reflected bright multicolored chips. A photographer had set up his tripod near the railing. They stopped to admire the view.

"So, where do we go for dinner?", Ivan asked.

"I propose the restaurant down the road, we ate an excellent sauce, last time", Sandro said.

"No, I have a better idea," Ivan said.

"Why do not say it right away, then?" Sandro said.

"Say what?" Ivan said.

"That you had already decided. You would have spared me the trouble."

That's that, the fuse had been lit. The three feared that, but basically they were expecting it.

"What do you think?" Sandra said to Umberto.

"About what?"

"About what is happening, about this unbearable situation", Sandro shouted.

"I don't think there's anything particularly strange between us," Umberto quietly said.

"Yeah, for you everything is always all right, as long as no one asks you to make decisions . . . it's ridiculous", Sandro yelled.

"Unbearable, indeed", Ivan turned to Umberto, who nodded, "how do you justify your attitude?"

"What are you talking about?" Sandro said.

"Oh great, now you're pretending you don't understand. But, we came here together, right?"

"So?" Sandro said.

"Right. Then explain yourself: what is this urge to make it on your own? Why don't you come down to the lake with us?"

"It 'simple", Sandro said, and then shouted: "I'm fed up with arguing for any nonsense, okay?".

When Ivan was restless, he fell into a series of seemingly inconsistent tics: first, a rapid search in his hair, then he brushed the collar of his shirt to verify the solidity of the buttons, eventually he tested the consistency of the buckle on the belt of his trousers. The sequence was repeated several times without the slightest variation.

"It's nine o'clock, I think we should get going if we want to find a free table", cautiously suggested Umberto.

—

Sandro walked towards the path that led to the chamois. In a plastic bag he had placed bread, salami, and a beer, a knife and some paper towel.

When he put his head out of the sleeping bag, at seven o'clock, his companions were still asleep. He came out of the bag and lit a cigarette, and watching his comrades he could not help but think that things were not going right.

He vigorously climbed the slope, managing to keep a sustained pace for a good while. A sign at the beginning of the route, informed that it would take not less than two hours to the average climber to cover the entire distance.

Among the loose stones that paved the initial stretch of the path, he noticed brown balls of manure that the sun was baking and changing in gold. He also noticed that the silence became more present, as he climbed: crackles, hisses and calls betrayed the presence of small invisible animals. Sandro picked up a sturdy stick as a support and to open his way into the parts where the vegetation was thicker. On the park's map the path was indicated by a slender red thread.

His initial vigour began to decrease, his breath became short and laborious, so Sandro decided to take a break. He slipped into a green space, he lied down on the ground among the grass and immediately a crowd of insects appeared around his sweaty body. He drew large and prolonged breaths of the fresh and fine air, until dizziness caught him. He took off his glasses and laid them on the grass.

The thought of his comrades left down in the valley caught him again. Not that he regretted the decision, basically they were not children, they would surely be able to organize their day without him. What annoyed him most, was that Ivan showed unprovoked animosity, which he considered unjust, against him, and Umberto's passivity. Despite being forty-five years old, Ivan had remained a spoiled brat. Had it not been for Umberto, who had assumed the burden of organizing his life, anticipating his wishes and satisfying them without question, Ivan would be lost. And he was baffled by Umberto's resignation, by his surrender without protesting.

Some noises and rustles of bushes broke the plot of his thoughts. When the clatter drew nearer, Sandro leaned forward to look. From a fissure in the branches he saw the muzzle of a cow that crossed his eyes. They stared at each other through a green fence that protected both, without making a decision. It would have been easy for the cow to break down the wall of branches that protected him, and continue its way. After all, he was the intruder up there.

Fortunately, the cow ignored him and continued to graze with its phlegmatic walk. Soon after, however, a disturbing thought came into Sandro's mind: what if I go astray, if I lose the trail? To exorcise that fear he suddenly stood up and recovered his way, taking care not to lose sight of the traces of red and white that marked the trail.

———

There was crowding around the enclosure of the wolves. Adults and children were leaning over the railing to track the movements of the pack and the games of the cubs. The soft chatter was dominated by the incessant buzz of flash lights. Ivan was part of that blaze, while Umberto was standing on the sidelines, with his back to the wolves.

The attention of the tourists was magnetized by the anxious wandering of an isolated wolf, at the edge of the community. Alone, without daring to approach, they said it had been chased away from the pack for daring to challenge the dominant male.

"We should do the same thing, what do you think?", Ivan said.

"What are you talking about?" Umberto said.

"About our friend, the lonely wolf, who, otherwise", Ivan sneered.

"Well . . . I do not know,", Umberto said whining, "you're kidding, right?"

Ivan did not reply, he turned toward the fence and took pictures of the man who, at that moment, had entered the enclosure and was spreading everywhere the food for the wolves. The drone of flash lights thickened, along with the exclamations of surprise. The wolves appeared to have lost their wildness and natural distrust of man, as the guard was wandering inside the area as if in a hen house. It was sad to see the wolves reduced to a harmless pack of dogs, but all this had a great effect on the tourists.

Umberto came close to Ivan, who continued excitedly to take pictures, especially when the exiled wolf passed beneath them. They saw the animal with the lost gaze parade melancholy. It passed very close. Despite its comfortable captivity, its appearance evoked images of savage pride. After a while the two lost interest in the show. They went off the fence and headed towards the nearby parking lot.

"What now?" Umberto said.

"You're asking me?"

"You know, I thought we could reach the village and . . ."

"To do what?"

"I do not know, I could think about it, in the meantime we could move, if you like, what do you think?"

"I think it's bullshit . . . think of a better idea."

They sat in the car and waited, not knowing for what.

"Do you think we should tell him?", Umberto said.

"What?"

"About the two of us."

Ivan stirred: hair, shirt collar, buttons, buckle of his pants. He did not answer, he looked into Umberto's eyes, but without a shadow of hostility, almost begging for a response from him, a decision whose gravity put him in front of impassable crossroads.

"Be quiet," Umberto said, "if you do not want to . . ."

"What where you saying about the village?"

"We could go get something in a bar, have a sit at a table and . . ."

"And?"

"Well, nothing, we could enjoy the shade . . . watch people going by . . . walking, things like that . . . nothing special . . ."

Ivan started up the engine while muttering between his teeth "nothing special".

"So . . . You did not answer," Umberto said.

"To what?"

"About us . . . whether it is appropriate to speak to . . ."

———

Since he was on his way, Sandro had not crossed with other people, and more than an hour had passed since he had met the cow. He kept his eyes down. The fear of getting lost had never left him since he was back on march. When he raised his head, a big man going down cluttered the path with his size. He wore a checked shirt, short pants, a long grizzled beard, a little hat and he seemed a mystic. In his right hand he brought a stick, and he wore ordinance boots.

"Have you seen the chamois, sir?" Sandro asked.

"Many," replied the big man, "but I've seen them from far away: they were scared and ran away. You know, where man arrives . . . If I were a chamois, I would as well run at the sight of a man."

Sandro could feel in his words a resentful vehemence.

"The fact is that one climbs up here without having, let's say, that . . . religious sense, I am talking about the religion of silence, which drives a man to climb, to isolate himself, to feel in harmony with what surrounds him."

The big man stopped, it seemed that the silence just mentioned was there, discrete and palpable, a demiurge who coordinated with unparalleled craftsmanship the rustling, the calls, the sound of the wind, the electric hum of insects and, from below, the bells that marked a dilated time. The big man was listening.

"You'll see, you will see by yourself, when you will be up there. I heard people screaming at the chamois . . . be certain they are not coming back so easily over there . . . Well, it takes little to break the spell . . . Where man arrives, he offends, disfigures, destroys, destroying himself. One can hit an animal scaring it to death and terror will be a more tremendous deterrent than of a shot, and this could result in a minor chance of survival . . . Do you follow me?"

"Oh, yes, sure."

"Listen . . . Let this silence invade you, be invaded by the miracle that still endures on these mountains."

There was a prolonged silence, the big man took a deep breath and wandered around with his eyes.

"Now I have to leave you, but go ahead, and remember: the silence. When you will be on the peak, shut up and listen to it."

Sandro saw the big man disappear into the valley. He resumed his journey, reflecting on the words of the big man and disregarding the direction he was taking. It repeated as a paternal recommendation: "listen to the silence . . . Listen", almost like a protective mantra.

When it became clear that he was no longer following the red and white trail, he had traveled so long a stretch than he could not retrace his steps. He turned towards the valley, observed the peak and felt alone.

"I lost the trail," he murmured.

He wiped the sweat coming down in streams and noticed that he no longer had his glasses.

"This too . . ."

He began to feel anxiety like a dull premonition.

"What now, I lost the glasses . . . and who knows where."

Despite everything, he felt still like climbing on. Confident in his shaky sense of direction, he resumed his journey, he missed his glasses and a bit of forces, but his determination did not leave him disheartened. "Are you sure you want to continue", he doubted, "alone and on a path not marked? And if you really got lost?" He thought that, in circumstances like these, a cellular phone would have been useful, but he hated that gadget.

The path he was running now seemed not very different from the marked one. Only silence now seemed to refer the echo of a panic hostility which he felt directed against him. He stopped at the foot of a large oak tree, he crouched with his knees between his arms and instinctively began to rock himself. He rocked for long recalling the words of the big man, listening to his fear, suspended between the carrying on and returning back to the valley. "I have not come this far to go back", he thought, "I'll go on."

This spur made him stand up and resume the journey. However, the painful sense of isolation was increasing. Silence emphasized the noises. He smelled the air and climbed the last stretch. He found himself in a clearing dotted with bushes. On crossing the grass he noticed the presence of broken twigs all of the same length. He followed the trail of twigs that looked like bleached bones and not very tall in the grass he noticed the presence of casts of mud hardened by the sun. "They look like footsteps", he thought.

As a matter of fact he recognized the footprints of a deer. While he was walking, bending to look the footsteps more closely, he felt his heart beating fast and his breath broken by a hold gripping his chest. He discovered other footprints, he dug his fingers into them and felt their borders. They had the shape of a foot, a solid, broad foot with four fingers. He muttered between his teeth the word "bear" fearing that the murmur could turn into a roar, scatter around and awake animals and ghosts lurking behind every tree, bush or rock.

The panic pushed him into an irrational escape. Pursued by fear, he jumped over branches and rocks, he crossed over bushes, jumped over ditches and humps of the ground, and in five minutes he found himself at the bottom, where the trail divided. He stopped, upset. He recognized the place and found the spot. He looked for his glasses: he found them and put them on . . . Now he could see better.

—

Dinner and the rest of the evening were poisoned by silence. Ivan and Umberto sat at a table in the Bear Tavern and waited to be three to order.

"We always have to wait", Ivan said, and started as usual: hair, collar, buttons, buckles, but this time he added the nose, who knows why.

"He can't be late," Umberto soothingly said, and looked around trying to escape from the dreary atmosphere that was gathering around their table.

He just couldn't bear another awful night : they were on holiday, for Christ's sake, they had come to the mountains to relax, and instead it seemed that he had fallen in the middle of two armed trenches, and he was to act as a target of Ivan's whims and intolerance, and of Sandro's hairy tolerance, by whom he felt treated like an idiot. Right as for Ivan, Umberto thought, of whom he had decided to take the responsibility, to "carry that cross", as his mother would say . . . "But not tonight, please". He wanted to keep away from all that for that night . . .

A thin and lanky blond boy, who had just come in, caught his attention: very short hair, a blue tank top that left uncovered his white shoulders, a tattoo on his arm and a piercing in his lower lip. From his shorts two hairy stilts came out. On his feet a pair of Nike shoes.

"He could be twenty years old", Umberto thought, "and the beard suits him very much, he is really nice". That ray of light was exactly what he needed, Umberto thought, and perhaps he would resolve his evening. Yes, but what about Ivan? He should have invented a credible excuse to stand up and above all to escape the web of grievances and resentments with which Ivan would besiege him. He could not pretend that he wasn't there and abandon him or, worse, tell him: "Do you see that boy, well, I bid you farewell, I found someone better".

He thought about that for a long time, and Ivan asked him what he was thinking.

"Nothing."

"You haven't uttered a word for ten minutes . . . You'd rather say you don't want to tell me."

"But nothing, I tell you, I don't think about anything."

"When you act so . . .", hair, collar, buttons, buckle.

Ivan looked around as if an insidious enemy were hiding somewhere, and then he thought that if he could not have control over Umberto's thoughts, then everything could happen, even that he was planning to leave him.

"Won't you tell me what you are thinking?"

"I've already told you: nothing."

Hair, collar, buttons, buckle, and then again hair, collar, buttons, buckle.

"Just stop that, you look like a puppet."

When Sandro joined them, Ivan was shamelessly giving performing his favourite obsession.

"Sorry for being late, have you ordered yet?"

"Oh, come, we would never do that," Ivan said.

"You're finally here," Umberto said.

"It's not my fault, and I'm still upset for what happened to me."

"Have you met the black man?" Ivan said.

"More or less . . . If you wish, I'll tell you."

"Oh, well, now we know how to spend the evening," Ivan said, while Sandro took sit in front of Umberto.

Umberto felt relieved. If Sandro could catalyze Ivan's attention, that would give him time to work out a strategy to escape.

The waiter came to take the orders but no one spoke. They just crossed eyes with suspicion.

"What are you having?"

"I'm not very hungry," Umberto said, "but I'll have what you are having," he said to Ivan. Then he quietly stood up and took a few steps towards the bench.

"Where are you going?" Ivan said.

"I'm taking a little walk, meanwhile you order, I'll be right back."

Ivan quivered: hair, collar, buttons, buckle.

Sandro, meanwhile, had begun to narrate his misadventure, and Ivan was pretending to listen. Sandro explained and Ivan stared in the empty space, Sandro got excited and Ivan looked for Umberto, Sandro had found his glasses and Ivan . . . hair, collar, buttons, buckle.

Who was that guy, that blond boy, Umberto was talking with?

—

The torments Umberto had to suffer in the next two days culminated with Ivan's decision to dump him for a whole day to accompany Sandro in his decision to climb the pass of the "Passo della Nevaia", two thousand five hundred meters high. "Anyway you won't be alone, I leave you with your boyfriend", Ivan told Umberto when he announced his decision. Umberto knew that was his way of punishing him, because Ivan would never have such an idea, his sloth would not let him.

Ivan did not precisely understand what Umberto found in that pale blond boy, in those four bare bones held together by a little flesh and tendons. Ah, maybe it was because he was a foreigner, a potato-eater who used to have cappuccinos for lunch and mayonnaise and other junk food for breakfast, who used to bath in the river and dry naked in the sun, and fortunately some caring mothers had stopped him. Umberto had not even tried to protest, he had merely wished him a good day and had assured him that he would have survived. And that had thrown Ivan into despair and utter anger. At least he could have shown a bit of suffering, at least a little jealousy. Nothing, Umberto showed he did not give a fuck, as they say.

The troubles, for Sandro, began early, when it came to convince Ivan to get out of the sleeping bag. It was six o'clock and the walk up to the Passo required four hours of walking. Sandro had tinkered all the afternoon of the day before with the park map, calculating to break up the walk in four stages, and snags apart—and could not help but think of Ivan—it would take five full hours, since the last stretch was severely uneven, and they would have to climb with bare hands.

After just half an hour's walk, Ivan found absurd the idea of having being involved in such a trek, although Sandro had pointed out that the idea was his, and that the reason why he, Ivan, was there now, had remained sleeping in the valley. The allusion terribly annoyed Ivan, but he could not execute its obsession—hair, collar, buttons, buckles—for the mere fact that he was holding a stick with his right hand.

"I would be grateful if, for the rest of the day, you could avoid naming that person."

"It will be difficult, since there are the two of us alone."

"Then, please talk about something else, if you do not mind."

"Oh, for me I can keep my mouth shut all the way, I do not know if you would be able to do likewise."

"What do you mean?"

"Nothing, please, I'm just saying that maybe you should concentrate a bit more on what surrounds you, maybe . . ."

"What?"

"Nothing, forget it."

Ivan wanted to stop and asked Sandro whether he agreed.

"Take your time, I will not run away."

Ivan sat down and put his stick on the floor: hair, collar, buttons, buckle. It had started really badly, Ivan thought. All the same, with someone like Sandro . . . But how did he dare to tell him to keep his mouth shut, damn it! All this was crazy . . . unbelievable . . . absurd, and moreover he had not even stopped, leaving him alone. And what if he needed help?, If he felt not well? He went away, not even looking around to ask whether all was right. And if he decided to go back down? What would he say? He would go wild with joy . . . well, he would give him no satisfaction, no sir.

"Come on you, lazy one", Sandro shouted, "you've got a long way to grind."

Ivan got up grumbling and tried to move on. What had he screamed? He seemed to understand something like 'street food', 'way to go'. He did not need to tell him what to do, he knew himself.

While Sandro preceded him, Ivan was working out all the possible variations of the phrase which he seemed to grasp, in order to reach the composition of the most complete, that is, the most offensive. He stopped all of a sudden, dropped his stick and: hair, collar, buttons, buckle. "You have a long way to grind": that was it. However, for once, he allowed himself the luxury of doubting of himself, because the sentence had been said, yes, but from far away, and the voice saying that phrase in his mind was not Sandro's, it was not a man's voice, it rather was the voice of an angry woman . . . Goodness knows

—

The waitress moved to Umberto's table and smiled.

"What would you like, sir?"

"A decaf cappuccino with no foam, and a croissant with jam".

"We only croissants with cream."

"Then . . . a *Fiesta*."

"Sorry, we only have *Buondì*", the girl replied, sincerely sorry, "if you wish, I can serve you a slice of pie, it's fresh, you know, made last night."

"Forget it, okay just the cappuccino, but half-warm, I beg you, with no cream."

The idea to start the day without croissants and jam annoyed him. To chase away the resentment he leafed the newspaper through, the only one who he had found, and it was not his newspaper. Despite these annoying setbacks, Umberto strived to maintain a neutral mood, tried to smile at the girl who served him his cappuccino, and pretended to show interest in what the newspaper reported of the world.

He had an appointment with Friedrich. Oh dear, an appointment was perhaps a strong word, because between them there had not been a real agreement, they just said "see you", that's all, and despite the fact that he had stayed at the table in the bar during the last two days, he hadn't even see Friedrich's shadow.

He only knew that Friedrich was German, that his mother was Italian, that his parents divorced, that he used to come down to Italy to spend part of his holidays with his mother and his new boyfriend. His house was just outside the village and every day Friedrich came there for shopping.

He also told him that in the village he did not know anyone and that he was boring.

Friedrich had not spoken about girls, and this seemed a good start to Umberto.

From his point of view, he would have liked to screw with him, despite the looming presence of Ivan.

The wait, during the days that followed their meeting at the Bear Tavern, was full of elaborate fantasies of seduction, Umberto's unusual behaviour was noticed by Ivan, who could do nothing else but asking account of it, obtaining from Umberto just triumphant silences and allusions. Ivan's unsteady certainties suggested that the veil of pretence had fallen on them, that it was not about his infatuation with the blond one, and that Umberto's nostalgic abandonment to fleeting memories, a certain melancholy sweetness excluded him, concealing folds of Umberto's temperament which he had never had access to.

Umberto, for his part, had found himself saddled with a role that was not his, and that was quite enough.

With a signal of his hand, Umberto called the girl's attention.

"Yes?"

"An espresso with a splash of milk . . . decaf"

"Coming."

The newspaper had been looked at a couple of times, the news was the same in the same pages, and of Friedrich there was nothing else than what Umberto remembered of him: sneakers, a tank top, tattoos and piercings and everything else.

The girl came back, put the cup on Umberto's table and asked if he needed anything else.

"What time does the disco open?"

"At ten p.m. during the week, later on Saturdays and Sundays, around midnight."

"There is a cinema in the village?"

"No, unfortunately, the nearest is thirty kilometers far, across the lake, I'm sorry."

"For the newspapers is the same thing, I guess?"

"I do not know what to tell you, sir, I'm sorry, but you know . . . it's always like this all year long, even in summer, only a few newspapers come up here."

"I understand . . . never mind."

The girl walked away, head down. Umberto saw her chatting with a guy in a white jacket and bow tie. He saw that the man shook his head and shrugged his shoulders.

When he turned to check the road Umberto saw Friedrich walking embraced to a girl, a brunette, he saw that he kissed her again and again, that he took her face in his hands and caressed her hair. He saw that they smiled to each other; he saw the abyss that separated him from Friedrich and felt himself dissolve in the crash that exploded in his chest.

—

"Why are you so quiet?", Sandro asked without any aggressive intent.

Ivan simply did not answer, he looked into Sandro's eyes, indeed he stared at him as if seeing him for the first time.

It was true, for about two hours he had not opened his mouth, he had not complained, he had not asked for unscheduled stops.

"It is better to stop," Sandro said, "in a while the hardest stretch will begin, it is better to recover strength."

They sat facing each other, Sandro wiped off the sweat that dripped abundant, Ivan put down the stick and, unbeknown to Sandro, he reviewed twice the sequence which, now more than ever, he felt he could not do without.

"We should be very careful from now on, the trail is lost and there will only be rocks to support us, and the abyss on the right and on the left."

"It seems that you know the path well," Ivan said, breaking a monastic silence.

"I've just studied the maps."

"Yeah", Ivan said, "You like studying, don't you?"

Sandro did not understand the meaning of the question.

"Of course, you always liked studying, that's why you were the teacher's darling."

"What are you talking about?"

"Oh, nothing . . . nothing, don't take any notice of that."

As a matter of fact Sandro ignored Ivan's last words believing that, having used up any excuse to be able to complain and to put on others the guilt of being alive and not only interested in Ivan, he was looking for new excuses, new and more imaginative excuses, if possible, than those he usually used.

Sandro searched in his rucksack and pulled out two sandwiches.

"There you go."

"Thanks, I'm not hungry" Ivan said, almost spelling.

"As you wish, but remember that this is the last stop, and I'm planning to get on the top with or without you."

Ivan stared at him as before and Sandro felt a shiver down his neck, as if that look condensed a hatred that could not be expected from Ivan.

"Would you pass me the flask? Sandro asked.

"Take it yourself."

The stop lasted about half an hour. For the rest of the time they would not speak; Sandro took advantage to take a look at the maps, Ivan continued with the silent and obscure work that had accompanied him for hours.

"I say it is better to set off again," Sandro said, breaking an awkward silence even for him.

Ivan did not reply, he made a gesture with his hand as to say "go ahead", he bent to pick up the stick and followed Sandro staring at his neck. The terrain was very rough and the stick was a hindrance, so Ivan left it on a rock thinking to retrieve it on the way back.

"There are only three hundred meters left, but look there", Sandro said thinking aloud.

"Are you speaking to me?"

"I said that there are only three hundred meters left, but, Good Heaven, look there."

"My primary school teacher used to say the same, now that I think of it," Ivan said.

"What are you talking about, are you kidding?"

"Not at all, now I remember it well, very well indeed."

"What do you remember?"

"My primary school teacher and her habit of repeating certain phrases, always the same: 'You've got a long way to grind" was one, the other was "Good Heaven", she always said that when scolding a child, and it is likely that she meant that not even God, in His infinite goodness, could do anything for the ignorance or the stupidity of the unfortunate in turn."

"What a weird idea, but how did you come to think of it?"

"It was you who made me remember."

"It sounds ridiculous, but it is so."

Sandro stared at the peak, he stumbled on the stones, holding to spikes of rock and avoiding looking at the bottom and back. He could feel Ivan's breath and smiled thinking of Ivan and his teacher.

"Also my teacher used to say "You've got a long way to grind", Sandro said.

"Really?"

"You had to see her," Sandro said, "she was very tall, and all her hair was white and very short and . . ."

"She looked like a man", Ivan interrupted.

"Yeah . . . and she even had a thick hair, which she used to shave, and we called it whiskers. Look, we used to say, the teacher has shaved . . . aaah . . ."

Ivan raised his head and saw Sandro hanging in the air, clinging to a rock edge, trying unsuccessfully to find a foothold for his feet.

"Help me . . . do something, Christ, don't stay there stock-stiff!"

"Even now, as then, the same arrogance," Ivan said.

"But what the hell . . . help me . . . and stop talking . . . raving bullshit."

"Of course I'll help you, Biolcati Alessandro", Ivan said, pronouncing Sandro's full name, "but first you must apologize to me."

"For what . . . damn it?", Sandro screamed in terror, still dangling.

"I recognized you, Biolcati, the teacher's darling, the most perfidious, the most wicked, the most malicious of the class second A, primary school "Carducci" . . . You don't remember me, do you?, But I remember of you. I'm Bollati Ivan, the next after you in the school list. You loved mocking me when the teacher Starnazza Italia bid me in the corner . . . how much you loved humiliating me, and how much you loved tormenting me . . . do you remember, Biolcati . . . well now it's my turn, Bollati Ivan's turn, to have fun . . . it seems right, don't you think?"

"Please . . . don't do that . . . help me . . . many years have passed . . . I don't remember anything . . . please . . ."

"It's a pity it was you who reminded me of that, with the phrase "you've got a long way to grind". You were right, teacher Starnazza repeated that often . . . Dear Biolcati, we had the same teacher, but it seems you had forgotten that."

"What do you want . . . me to . . . say, I'm sorry and . . . oh, shit . . . help me, and can't . . . I can't find . . . a poin . . ."

"Farewell, Biolcati", Ivan softly said as he saw Sandro's body falling down. "Say hello to teacher Starnazza if you see her . . . How much have I hated you, Biolcati . . .", he sighed.

———

Umberto watched the starry night lying in his sleeping bag, counting shooting stars: you never know, future could be better than that holiday. Ivan was dozing, from time to time he gave turns in the bag and moaned incomprehensible words. Umberto tried to call him.

"Are you sleeping?"

No reply. He tried to shake him and eventually Ivan turned.

"What's up?"

"I cannot sleep."

"Just try", Ivan said, "just close your eyes and count the sheep."

"I'm trying to count the stars, but apparently it's not working."

"The fact is that you do not move, you do not get tired, you spend all the time sitting at a table, that's why at night you can't sleep . . . you have to do exercise, you must get tired, just like me."

"Yeah, and risk to lose my life?"

"Don't think about it, it was an accident that could happen to anyone . . . but it is not certain that it should happen to you . . . try to sleep."

It was the last night they spent in the park, the next day they would return to their town. And without Sandro, Umberto thought.

"But how did it happen, really?"

"No, please, again this story, I have told you a dozen times: it was an accident, how should I tell you, an accident, he couldn't find a toehold and slid downhill, and I couldn't do anything to help him, I was too far away in that moment, okay? There is nothing else to say, it was an accident, only an ill-fated accident . . . now sleep!"

Sandro's death had upset poor Umberto. But before that, and perhaps more, the stark disillusionment about Heinrich hurt him, the open wound was still there to testify that something had gone forever, and that included Ivan, their relationship. Nothing is forever, that maxim had been the helm of his life, and nevertheless the too predictable events of his life, until then, had preserved him from sudden surges and cruel blows. Death and pain were now streaking the surface of colorless certainties never put to the test.

"What time do we leave, tomorrow?" Umberto said.

"We'll take it easy, we'll wake up at eight, you'll collect the stuff and put it in the car, we'll have breakfast and then we go. Ah, before leaving we must go to the police, there are still some formalities that need to be attended to."

"What are you planning to do, after?"

"After when?"

"When we get home . . . when you will be in your house and I in mine."

"I do not understand, what do you mean?"

"I think we should call it a day, don't you think?"

"Finally you got it. This obsession of yours to know more, more and more, about how things have gone, was starting to get on my nerves."

"Is that what you think?"

"Yes, you were starting to be intolerable."

"You think I'm talking about what happened to . . . poor Sandro?"

"And what else, otherwise, you haven't done anything else for days."

"Yeah . . ."

Umberto thought that the return journey was going to be very long, that the city, his house, his job were not the going to be the same, and that he had had enough of Ivan's ignorance.

He thought long about that, and decided that, maybe, it was better to count the stars.

Half-serious bewilderment and passion of an unrepentant satyr

. . . .

Those nymphs . . . I want . . . forever.
So clearly
Vibrates their slight hue that slowly turns in the air
in a thick sound.
Is it following a dream?
(from "The Afternoon of a Faun" by S. Mallarmé)

I'VE ALWAYS CONSIDERED DREAMS VERY important, and as much important are daydream frenzies, better still I can state that frenzy is the natural condition of my mind.

During the time I have even worked out a theory, not that original I must say, which identifies and classifies two kinds of frenzy: the good one and the bad one. As far as I can remember about my naughty attitude, girls have always been the object of my good frenzy.

I still vividly remember how I used to get upset, as a beardless adolescent, by a pair of white knee socks wrapping up the tough calves of an unapproachable and crabby girl of my own age. Or the paralyzing ecstasy I got when another schoolmate of mine—we attended the comprehensive school—rushed into the classroom wearing a very tight dress, too short over the knees, and besides she had on a pair of nylon stockings wrapping her legs, that seemed molded by a divine sculptor.

Oh, how much have I suffered on such details, and how many summer afternoons sacrificed on the altars of Priamus and Eros, my ubiquitous companions and inspirers.

But the place of honour in my very personal Pantheon no doubt belongs to Pan and his court of nymphs.

Moreover, my job is my sentence, it appears to be my nemesis, since girls, together with their same age boy fellows, are the subject and object of my job: I teach Musical Theory and Solfeggio in a private school.

And last night I dreamed of the most pretty one.

It is often difficult for me to separate reality from imagination and dream. It's an effort I avoid with pleasure, even if, as today, I am obliged to take my reality amongst the reality of the rest of the world.

The students look at me as I enter the classroom.

"Good morning!"

I take a seat, I sign the register and give a glimpse to the students still standing, waiting for me to say: "Sit down!"

I stare at the little girl of my dream: slim, slender, her unripe breast, one can see a slight swelling under her shirt. I can see the outline of her top: does she wear a bra? Her face naturally smooth, not a pimple—she takes a quick look at me, I cannot define: anxiety? Expectation? Is she observing me? What is that look asking of me? What is she expecting from me: a smile? A grimace? I almost feel like show her the tongue, just like a kid.

She entered into my secret, unspeakable night dreams, through the door of love frenzy.

My dream suggested to kiss her on the cheek, to hold her tight by my side—I embraced her shoulders.

Just like when, as a teenager, I used to walk along the paths of a park. At night, in winter, it was dark and cold . . . Ah, it was winter.

Tight by my side a girl, sixteen years old, the first one: kisses, caresses. We remained close for hours, we kissed each other till our lips swelled up. And hands that hesitated, that rummaged, that did not dare. Guilty ejaculations in my underpants: (she) "What's happened?", (me) "Nothing".

Yet, something did happen. The explosion of desire, the overwhelming fury of the first sex, guilt lied in wait.

And now this little girl. Her body, almost a woman even if unripe, slender but ready to blossom, perfumed of delight, far from me, untouchable. And I dreamed of that body, that shape, her voice, the warmth: she stayed by my side effortlessly, with no fear, no space between her and me, just the seam tying up our bodies . . .

I would like to stand up and kiss her as in my dream—I brushed against her cheek, I attempted a kiss but we were not coordinated: impossible synchrony? I stand up, wandering about in the room. I observe their back, her back: carved in marble, hips smoothed down . . . what a waste of grace—I imagine her in my arms, with my eyes I travel along her hips, I slide on her shoulder and get to her neck, to her amber cheeks: I imagine to brush against her lips, softly, with fear. Am I too old for these lips? Are my hands too rough for this unaware sensuality?

There was more in my dream: many people, adolescents, my equals as for desires and daydreaming fancies—it is there, among the school desks, that the frozen clot of the primitive Eros begins to come undone, as if suddenly it woke up from a long lethargy that meant oblivion. At that age the curve of a thigh is like a sudden intuition, the curve of a breast makes us scream in agony, makes us sleepless and anxious. The smell of the female chases us, the adolescents, exasperates us, exhausts us.

I speak, I smile, my pupils smile. Males are a little pathetic, sometimes disoriented, they ignore or pretend to ignore, they refuse to watch, refuse to look at themselves. Someone is struggling against the down coming up over his lips, some others cheat themselves with uncertain guttural sounds, and definitely they prefer playing tricks.

Females, on the contrary, oh . . . it seems they go around all over the place announcing they are transforming into precious, mysterious, delicate objects.

Objects to dream of, exactly, to be desiderated and envied, too.

They talk, they withdraw, they rule out. They have something more, inside, they know it, they tell each other about it, they carefully keep it: their secrets.

And males pretend to ignore that, they do not know they are going to square things up with those secrets. Do they know they will try to obtain what they lack from the girls? Is that how the final intention inserts into their minds, into my mind: violate them to get their secrets, subdue them to possess them? Is that how the terrible illusion, the rape, entraps us?—"I destroy your body, I humiliate it because it rules me out, rules us out". Is that so?

Beauty can be oppressive sometimes, unreachable, impossible to understand: the girl, her body, the plastic and not refined shape move my despair.

Not in my dream. We laughed, we talked, we were a couple close in intimacy. Were we happy?

I come back to my desk, I listen to their voices. My students.

I can hear again my voice, in the dream—adult among teenagers, adolescent out of time: I am surrounded by confusion and . . . Suddenly I take notice of it, I look into my pants, they are dirty, stained with blood: has something that does not belong to me opened out between my legs? Menstruation! My blood is coming out, but out of what hole, what wound? It is not purple, it is not intense and mysterious: diluted, faded, just a nuance drawing the profile of my thighs on the pants . . .

Theirs, on the contrary, is secret, hidden.

I look at the males and ask myself: do they know the blood? Can they understand it? If you, as for necessity once happened to me, enter a women's toilette, that prohibited and mythical gynaeceum, you can see it.

I entered a women's toilette one afternoon, I locked the door and pissed. I thought I was violating that place with my presence. I entered as a stranger, in exile from my adolescent fantasies. And I saw it. Abandoned in the bin, modeled, preserving intact the wrinkles and the reliefs of the pubis that had given hospitality to it. A slight fold in the middle, tiny lips slightly open in a red smile. It was small, a little bigger than a plaster. It appeared to have been abandoned there as a precious proof, maybe with the same pleasure girls have in showing around their fluent and smooth hair, together with the pride of their not yet violated breasts, sometimes bulky and attractive. It was sort of tender, and suggested some hypothesis to me. Whom it belonged to? It was not easy to discover, I should have gone sniffing around like a hound, smelling lost traces.

And in my dream the menstruation was mine. And I was on a footrest. Was I acting? I was performing as sometimes I do when I am in front of my choir. My role should be clear when I am in front of the choir, I think. But it not always is, the sexual I mean.

I walk again around the room and meanwhile I look at her, the girl of the dream. I recall all those who have been here, many of them. I recall those, as her, I have desired, I have imagined to possess, to rape, but it always is the same story, the same despair.

The same of the time when, as a boy, I watched, not seen, the discreet, gracious, soft pacing of a tough teenager's body—desire, repressed fury, pain in the body; but everything remained there, in the body and in the mind, and the unspeakable obsessions started again persecuting me.

I used to confess that to a priest, there were many of them, each time a different one to avoid making known my teenager obscenities: desire sin guilt punishment expiation desire . . . this was the circle that always entrapped me.

Now there is no priest, but a deep gap remains, a hole other women could not fill. I try to fill it imagining today's girls, but I should rather put back the clock in my mind and accelerate the girls' one: seducing them in pectore is only thing left to me to do.

Moreover as a seducer . . . I have not got the technique, therefore I just try to seduce their young and absorbing minds.

I review them in the calm moments, as if recalling their images could awaken who knows what storms in my senses and my spirit. I return young, I mix myself up with their young appearances, accomplice of their secrets. I imagine I can furtively get in their bedrooms, I hide myself behind their wardrobe, under their bed. What do they do when they remain alone? What does the girl of my dream think when she remains alone, lying on bed or on a sofa looking around? Has she discovered that point? Does she ignore it? Does she accurately keep it for other hands, different from her own? Has she traced the borders of her body, covering it with swift, discreet, astonished fingers? Does the bite torment her? Does the spasm of her young abdomen press her? Does she let go? I can imagine her emerge from the Whirlpool, astonished, aware. Day by day her body grows and she discovers new sensitivities: the ground of mysteries to share with the other girls is enlarging.

And I among them, as in the dream, with my male body and a fantasy of menstruation between my thighs. I can feel my confusion, my uncertainty—like the indecision of the dream, the impossible synchronism of a kiss on her cheek.

She is extremely shy, she does not dare to, she fears and so do I. So I play mixing up, trying to amaze them.

I try to imitate the males sometimes, trying to learn from them—in the dream I waited for a colleague to prompt my part while I was acting. It was not any colleague at all, but "that one", a sort of second father, a putative, kind-hearted, helpful father you can even make fun of, when you feel like to.

Learning to be a male again, then, to approach girls "again", insinuating on the same plane in their talks, in their teenager's attitudes, in their little disputes. They! Sometimes haughty, disagreeable, unreachable, incomprehensible. And, most of all, inviolable.

Meanwhile the hour is almost through, in a while I shall go out of the classroom.

In the dream I was a pupil, one among many. In the classroom—maybe a crypt, a presbytery in the place where the desk is meant to be—an acquaintance of mine: more clever than me in the art of seduction, younger than me, one who does not seem to have lost the thread of his still recent past. Stories of cheerful fucking, with no fears nor remorse, alone or in group. For me another galaxy. In the dream he showed to me little red and black candles, those candles you put on birthday's cakes.

My birthdays are printed on my face, among the hairs of my grayish beard. Also my thoughts and my mood are getting grey, but this does not seem to discourage my frenzies as an unfinished adolescent. I try every time, every year the same scenes, the same steps, the same inconclusiveness.

I stand by the girl's side, slightly behind her smoothed down nape of the neck. She is bent over her music exercise book carrying out a work, they all are carrying it out, diligently and I pretend to check its accuracy.

In my dream I got in front of the teacher and asked her if she would date with me. In reality, it has happened to me only once, with a colleague I had fallen in love with. It appeared to be a serious thing: I was crazy about her, languid and without the courage to propose—it seems an obsolete formula. All the tenderness, the expectation, all in a proposition: I would like to go around with you. And also the acceptance of her refusal, which I feared and which arrived, polite but firm. I melancholically licked my wound: just like when I was a boy.

Because, actually, rather than falling in love I was always sick of love. Absolutely disoriented by the melancholic languor, by the spleen that attacked me every time the sweetness of a girl's face touched me. I got sad because I already knew how it all would end: I would not have the courage.

After that, I got colder. Sex played its part, but the fear of suffering sealed me, as shut up in a crypt—maybe that in the dream, the crypt-classroom.

Every year I try again to recover, and then, here: the girl of the dream.

But is it really true that the bell of my complicate adolescence has definitely rang?

What now if I dare with her, "my little girl"? She could save me, help me search among the ruins.

I could tell her: "Listen, let's play a game, the game of falling in love. I want to learn and you will teach me. I will diligently follow you and I think I have too much to learn".

I stare for long at her ponytail. Someone asks for the time. In a while it will be over.

"In a while the bell will ring", I say.

I depart from the little girl, who is unaware of my confusion, and I seat back at my desk.

"For next week, repetition".

Even if they will not need it. They have nothing to repeat, as I have, but only to live.

The bell rings. I come out of my frenzy.